Little by Little

Little by Little

Syd Little

CANTERBURY
PRESS
Norwich

First published in 2004 by the Canterbury Press Norwich
(a publishing imprint of Hymns Ancient & Modern Limited,
a registered charity)
St Mary's Works, St Mary's Plain,
Norwich, Norfolk NR3 3BH

www.scm-canterburypress.co.uk

British Library Cataloguing in Publication data

A catalogue record for this book is available
from the British Library

ISBN 1-85311-595-9

Typeset by Rowland Phototypesetting Ltd,
Bury St Edmunds, Suffolk
Printed and bound in Great Britain by
Biddles Ltd, www.biddles.co.uk

CONTENTS

ACKNOWLEDGEMENTS
AND THANKS

Many thanks to my wife, Sheree, and Dominic and all my family and friends who mean so much to me and have reminded me about many of the stories I had forgotten; to Christine Smith and the team at Canterbury Press for believing in me enough to let me pen another book; to Chris Gidney and his family for writing and editing the book and encouraging me; to Sally Goring for all her support at CIE.

'Footsteps' song is sung by Daniel O'Donnell but the author is unknown. The author of the 'Looby Loo' song is also unknown, but if this is pointed out to me I will be very happy to credit him or her in the next edition of this book. Monty Python's 'Galaxy Song', is written by Eric Idle.

Further information

Action for ME: www.afme.org.uk
Christians in Entertainment: www.cieweb.org.uk
Details of Syd's gospel events: www.shorehillarts.co.uk

INTRODUCTION

They say it's the little things in life that really matter and I've certainly found this to be true through the years in my own journey. Of course, this probably sounds strange coming from one half of the famous comedy duo Little and Large, someone who has experienced the dizzy heights of fame and fortune.

Indeed, I know what it feels like to have more money than I could ever spend and to be able to buy anything I took a fancy to. I had more fans than I could wish for waiting just for me at the stage door after the show every night and the press have pursued me for years – sometimes they have caught me! Our Saturday night television series ran continuously for 14 years on the BBC and we've just celebrated 40 years in showbiz. Sometimes it seems like we've been famous forever. Funnily enough, I'm still stopped on the street by well-wishers and autograph hunters, though I think I'm more of a collector's item now!

Yet, a career of glamour and fun, money and popularity quickly fades when placed beside my personal life. Behind the laughter of a clown have been the real tears of tragedy and turmoil. Away from the sometimes unreliable reassurances of agents and managers, I've known the real ups and downs of a rocky personal life. Mine is a classic tale of huge success on the outside and desperate hardship on the inside – or is it?

Actually, I've had my fair share of calamity. My eldest son

died of a heroin overdose and my daughter was attacked and left to die. Accountants lost all my pension and the press told so many untrue stories about me. My younger son suffered from ME and Eddie, my friend and partner, was told that he would die if he didn't have a heart transplant. Like stepping stones through the river of my life, there have been plenty of wobbly ones that threatened to throw me off balance, straight into the murky water beneath.

Yet, rather than the big things in life, it is the little things that have kept me going and kept me sane in a mad world. My wife. My family. My friends. Most of all, my God. 'He's not little,' I hear you cry. 'He's a big God' and, indeed, that is true. However, he's made himself little enough to walk by my side every step of the way. Little enough to incline his ear to my lips as I utter yet another feeble prayer for help. Little enough to want to spend time with me and show how much he cares. Little enough to show how, together, we can turn each disaster into a success. That is just what he has done. My clouds are the ones with silver linings.

Little by little, I have seen the worst situations and the deadliest of circumstances slowly develop into springboards of opportunity. Little by little, I have moved shakily through the various seasons of my life. From the uncertainty of autumn and the terrifying cold of winter, the spring eventually arrives and the summer is promised.

Mine is an amazing story – a true story, an encouraging and inspirational story – but it is one that I couldn't have come through on my own, not without the little things in life to carry me onward. Come with me and I'll show you what I mean.

I

A MATTER OF LIFE
OR DEATH

I just couldn't move because something or someone was pinning me down. Bursts of bright, white light appeared and disappeared, enveloping me then plunging me back into darkness again. My mind was working of its own accord, my body felt detached. Surely I was dead and on my way to the great beyond.

When eventually I opened my eyes for a moment, the only things I could see were more lights. Hundreds of them, streaming over me as if a roadway had been painted on the ceiling.

It was the sharp pain in my left hand, caused by the slow insertion of a needle, that brought me back to reality. I heard the frantically creaking wheels of a trolley being pushed very fast before I opened my eyes and found myself staring at the brown rubber tube of a stethoscope and a set of coiled wires.

'Clear the way! Clear the way! Coming through!'

Who were they talking about?

'Open your mouth please, Mr Little.'

Unable to speak, I obeyed without a word and felt a skilful finger tuck a small object under my tongue before passing back into the world of dreams. My mind swam with confusion and nothing made sense.

For several days I hovered between what seemed to be life and death. It was as if I was part of some epic movie, but somehow deep inside I knew that this was for real and that I was probably going through the process of passing away. Actually, this wasn't far from the truth.

In the haze of my semi-conscious mind, various scenes began to play right in front of me. They say that when you are dying your life flashes before you and, looking back, it was just like that. Curiously, one of these dreamlike sequences was the last time that I had come face to face with death.

It was my own fault, but potholing in the hills in Derbyshire was a hobby for most teenagers in our town. I was no exception, but no expert either. 'The Chimney' is a very famous pothole in the Derbyshire hillside that lives up to its name. A small opening in a field leads down into a long, narrow chamber, 70 feet deep, that eventually arrives at the mouth of a huge cave.

Although we were with John and Chris – two older guys who seemed to know what they were doing – we ignored the fact that it was quite dangerous and that we were pretty inexperienced. It was February, and freezing, and we had spent over an hour exploring in the darkness of the lower chambers, equipped only with our torches. Having reached the floor of the cave, it was now time to get out. One by one my mates scrambled slowly up towards the entrance, using the rope to heave themselves skywards and out to freedom. As I saw the last pair of shoes disappear up into the blackness, it reminded me how awful it must have been for the small boys who were sent up chimneys to clean them in the Victorian era.

Now I was the last one left in the cave – it was my turn.

'Syd, hold on to the rope and we'll pull you up!' they shouted down.

I began to face the prospect of being hauled up the long dark tube of solid rock and took a small gulp to steady my nerves. I liked the going down, but I was never that keen on the going back up!

The rope had knots tied in it to make it easier to hang on to, but I was more than 60 feet off the ground when the rope suddenly swung to the side. I wondered for a moment whether the guys heaving me up on the rope had toppled sideways. Still clinging to the rope as it swung, my hands hit the side of the rock and I instinctively let go with a loud, 'Ouch!'

I fell several feet straight into the narrow, angular part of the pothole that had given it its famous name. I pushed my legs, shoulders and elbows outwards, jamming myself in the 'chimney'. If it hadn't been for this life-saving curvature of the pothole, I would have been like a pancake on the ground below.

I was bruised, cut and shaking with fear and cold. I was also soaking wet because water was running over the surface of the rock and, as I rested to get my breath back, freezing drips ran down my face.

Although a bit dazed, I heard the shouts from above, 'Syd! Syd! Are you OK?'

I was too shocked to speak for a while and the silence only served to cause further panic above ground. The shouts got louder and more frenzied. I tried to answer their cries, but my mouth and lungs were full of wet dust so I couldn't shout with any volume and I was using all my energy to remain spreadeagled in the vertical tunnel. I imagined with terror not being able to hang on for any length of time or staying entombed in the rock. Worse still, if the boulders supporting me gave way, I would have plummeted further down the shaft and I knew that this could happen at any moment.

The reassuring sight and sound of distant feet frantically hitting against the vertical tunnel above me brought some relief, but it took a while for Chris to reach me.

'Good grief. That was close! We thought you were a gonner!' he said when he finally reached me.

'So did I! How are you going to get me out of here?'

Another rope went around my waist and I was soon pulled up and out of the hole to safety by a very anxious bunch of guys. I lay at the top by the shaft, dazed and breathless, and stared at the handful of very red and scared faces peering down at me.

Back safe and sound at home, I decided not to tell my parents – I don't think they would have approved of my sense of adventure. I didn't go potholing again after that anyway.

These glimpses of events from long ago continued as my body lay in a hospitalized daze, occasionally waking up to discover myself surrounded by more wires, tubes and machines, only to drift back into dreamland again.

I was abruptly woken to my senses one night with a fearful noise coming from nearby. As I turned to see where the racket was coming from, my eyes focused on the flowery curtains of the cubicle next door. I could hear the medics' clipped tones, like something straight out of a medical drama.

'Clear!'

'Perdum! Perdum!'

'Clear!'

'Perdum! Perdum!'

It took me a while to realize what was happening, but when I did, I was filled with anxiety. The patient next to me was being resuscitated and for a moment I thought it was me. It must have been sheer panic that sent me back to sleep in spite of the commotion.

When I woke later the next day, I was shocked to see that the nearby cubicle was empty. The full realization of what had happened last night and where I was slowly began to dawn. I strained to sit up when a nurse with a big smile brought me a cup of sweet tea. She helped me with my pillows because I had so little energy. Her sympathetic beam said it all really and I could imagine her saying, 'We thought you were finished, but it's nice to have you back.'

As I sipped the warm brew, I began to feel grateful to be

alive and reflected on my life as a 52-year-old still in show-business.

One half of the famous comedy duo Little and Large for nearly 30 years at that point, I had had an interesting life, but surely now it was all going to change. Would I ever be well enough to work again?

As Little and Large we had enjoyed considerable fame and fortune. With a 14-year-long series on BBC1 behind us, we were still playing to packed houses wherever we went. There seemed no end to our popularity. I was the perfect stooge for Eddie's brilliant comedy characters and audiences loved our on-stage antics. With the roly-poly Eddie and the drain-pipe Syd, people who saw us were laughing long before we even opened our mouths and perhaps that was one of the secrets of our success.

When we did open our mouths, my job was to 'feed' the lines and create the timing for the quick-fire brilliance of Eddie's gags and superb impressions that literally had the audiences rolling in the aisles. The chemistry between us was magical and we would often know exactly what each other was going to say before we even spoke. However, while Eddie and I enjoyed a very successful public partnership, our private lives were quite separate as we pursued different interests.

I finished my tea, placed the empty cup and saucer on the bedside table and began to piece together a picture of me and Eddie Large backstage, just hours before the chain of events that had landed me in my present hospital predicament.

Having known Eddie for over 30 years at this point I knew his mood swings and when I arrived at the hotel I could tell he wasn't in a good frame of mind. Eddie could make me feel uneasy and I started to get uptight very quickly. I felt quite depressed and down as I went out on to the stage knowing that I wasn't quite with it.

Among the lights and echo of the PA, the laughs were coming thick and fast as we launched into our well-polished hour-long act. Then, for some reason, I missed an important cue line and Eddie's face changed to beetroot. Eddie, skilled as he is, managed to get out of the problem, turning the mistake into another laugh, but I knew I was in for a drubbing afterwards.

As I followed him down the hallway back to the dressing room, he made some cynical remark which made me even more stressed. He left me feeling dazed and near to tears.

As I put my suit in to the car, the rain began to pour down and I didn't savour the idea of the long journey back home to Torquay alone. I drove through the night with so many things going through my mind.

'I need this like a hole in the head.'

'Is it worth carrying on?'

'Have I got enough money to pack it all in?'

I had received a letter from Eddie a few weeks previously suggesting that we split up. 'I can do Little and Large in my sleep,' he said, going on to say that he wanted to go it alone. He had done some after-dinner speaking and enjoyed it so much he wanted to do some more.

After four or five hours of driving through the torrential rain, I eventually arrived home. I stumbled into bed, hoping I could sleep, but I just lay there in a state of distress.

'How did it go?' asked my wife in the morning.

'Terrible,' I admitted as I began to tell her how depressed I really felt.

'Well, at least you've got a day off,' she encouraged.

I was still feeling odd, but it was my job to lay the table for the family Sunday lunch, so, after a quick game of footie in the back garden with my son, I started to place the knives and forks in their proper places. Suddenly, a massive pain surged across my chest.

Whack! Like a lightning bolt it hit me and I was left fighting for breath. I stumbled into the kitchen where Sheree immediately saw how grey I was looking.

'Lie down and I will ring the emergency number for the doctor,' she advised.

After a quick call to the GP, Sheree came over and sat on the settee where I lay.

After a while, I was still not feeling any better and she called the surgery again.

'Don't worry, Syd. The doctor's on his way.'

When the GP arrived, Sheree said she was worried. He took one look at me and said, 'So am I', and called for an ambulance. The paramedics smiled in recognition of their local celebrity, but kept asking me how often the pains were coming. Still trying to be the funny guy, I asked if they had mistaken me for someone going into labour. In fact, the pain was so intense, it would not have surprised me had I given birth on the way to hospital. At one point, the pain caused me to drift off into my own little world and I felt a plastic mask being placed over my mouth. Apparently it was all pretty much touch and go, but it wasn't long before I was in the A&E department and in safe hands.

'Don't cross your legs, Mr Little,' said a disembodied voice outside my drifting thoughts. 'It's bad for your circulation.'

I looked up from my hospital bed and saw a male nurse standing over me. I then looked down at my feet to see them pulled tightly together. I did as I was told, separating them and trying, without success, to relax at the same time.

The nurse reached down and started to massage my feet. It tickled as he manipulated my toes and I felt strangely embarrassed. It was such an odd and intimate experience, but something that the nurse had obviously done hundreds of times before. It seemed to work, though, and I felt my stress levels subside.

'You've got a guest,' he smiled after a while. 'Shall I bring her in?'

When I saw my wife approach the bed, I didn't know whether to try to jump out of bed and hug her or burst into tears, but just the gentleness of Sheree's hand in mine was enough. I knew that she had been to see me many times over the past four days while I lay motionless in a haze of drugs in the intensive care unit of the cardiac department, but now I was sitting up in bed and chatting away with some cohesion.

'Sorry, Angel.'

'Nothing to apologize about, just take it easy and get yourself better,' said the woman whose wonderfully big blue eyes had inspired my nickname for her. Those eyes were now red with holding back the tears and I could see that the same terrible thoughts about my condition had been going through her mind, too.

'Try not to worry. Everything will be all right.'

I found it hard to believe her, but there was some consolation in her voice.

'Dominic's here.'

Sheree pulled back the curtain and Dominic, who we call our 'miracle boy', cautiously tiptoed in. I could see that Sheree was anxious as to how he would cope with the clinical paraphernalia of a hospital, but he sat on my clean white bed and began to ask the sorts of inquisitive but endless questions that six-year-old boys seem to specialize in.

We call him our miracle boy because, at the start of our marriage, we were told we couldn't have children. We had tried everything, from IVF treatment to some weird and wonderful diets, but nothing seemed to work. The only thing left was our prayers and even they had begun to fade a little over time. Then, suddenly, 13 years later, Dominic arrived! Sheree and I were ecstatic. As far as we were concerned, he could only have been the result of a miracle, so he has been known as our miracle boy ever since.

I tried to answer as many of Dominic's questions as possible until Sheree finally said, 'I think it's time we went home. Your dad looks tired.'

'I love you, Daddy', were his last words to me as they both said their goodbyes and gave me reassuring hugs. I was still unsure as to how ill I actually was and, as I watched them leave, I wondered if I would ever see them again.

Fears of an early death were pretty securely grounded in my mind. My mother had suffered a severe cardiac arrest only a few years previously. It was so forceful it had blown a hole in the wall of her heart. Auntie Jessie found her on the floor of her room and she was in such a bad way that the ambulance men wouldn't move her at first. They stabilized her, then got her to Wythenshawe hospital, but she died two weeks later.

Dad had also died of a sudden heart attack in 1964. He arrived back home from a fishing trip, gobbled down his tea, then ran all the way to the Labour Club because he'd missed the bus. When he got there, he ordered a pint and said, 'I've been waiting for this all day.' Then he lifted the glass to his lips and keeled over. He was only 50 years of age.

Now I was in hospital with the same condition, exactly 30 years later. I had already overstepped his 50 years by just a couple more. Maybe now it was *my* turn.

Lying in my hospital bed, I just couldn't get my mind free of such terrifying thoughts – they were going round and round like a record. I didn't want to die, but I was certainly resigned to the possibility of it. I knew it was only a matter of time before the next attack came and then that would be the end of it. Perhaps it would come tomorrow, perhaps tonight, perhaps even in the next 30 seconds.

Thoughts of God and questions of heaven whirled around my mind alongside worries of how Sheree and Dominic would cope without me. The thought of not seeing my six-year-old son grow up was too distressing and I decided it was time to pray.

Prayer was something that I had been familiar with since

my youth club days in Wythenshawe, Manchester. I had enjoyed going to church ever since I was a little lad at Sunday school. St Michael's and All Angels was just two doors away from us. Needless to say, I always claim that my mates and I were the 'angels'. Perhaps not!

Mum was the cleaner at the church. As a little boy, I would be amused to watch her dust the altar at great speed because there was a huge wooden cross hanging on a rope from the ceiling, and she was always frightened that it would fall on her while she was underneath it.

Every Friday night at the youth club was great fun as I mixed with all the local lads and lasses to play snooker at the church hall. Each evening would end with a sort of epilogue about how God cares for us and hears every prayer we utter. Youth club became a good place to hang out with other teenagers, but, when I discovered girls, the guitar and, eventually, showbiz, the whole church thing was sent flying out of the window. The entertainment business is like a religion in itself and there is no room for anything else. My Christian faith had recently been resurrected, however, and, lying here in hospital, it was more important to me than ever before.

Certainly God had looked after me in the last few days. The possibility that I could have suffered the heart attack in the middle of the night while driving home didn't bear thinking about. I could have crashed and died all alone at the side of the road.

I spent much time in the next few hours that followed talking to God, thanking him for getting me through them. I just chatted away and asked that, whatever happened next, would he please look after Sheree and Dominic. I felt a strange and warming peace inside, as if the answer 'Yes' had already been given and I didn't need to worry.

Strangely, I wasn't bothered about losing my career; perhaps for once in my life, it was the last thing on my mind. I

was convinced that I was on my way out and the only things
that mattered now were those closest to my heart.

On the other hand, I reasoned with myself, I was a comedian. As one half of Little and Large I had spent almost
every day of the last 30 years making people laugh, on stage,
on telly, even in the supermarket. Now I just couldn't think
of a single joke to cheer myself up. Eddie sent a card with a
funny message that made me laugh.

Laughter is certainly God's medicine – it can break through
almost anything eventually. Some light relief came from our
first ever television producer, Royston Mayoh, who rang
Eddie one day.

'When I read in the papers that one of you had suffered a
heart attack I assumed it was you Eddie! With the way you
work and your weight that wouldn't have been a surprise.
When you talk to Syd next, ask him if he's having the heart
attack on your behalf.'

When Eddie told me this story on the hospital telephone
the next day, I nearly fell out of bed laughing.

One of the greatest problems was trying to keep the press at
bay until we knew what the real situation about my medical
condition was. People in showbiz are never supposed to be
ill and the fear of losing future bookings always looms omin-
ously. My management tried to keep the story under wraps,
but news like this gets leaked fast. One reporter was apparently pestering for an interview and even tried to smuggle
himself into the hospital complete with camera to try to get
a picture of me in my most forlorn state. Fortunately, the
hospital was wise to this and managed to uncover his plot.
Caught trying to photograph me through a window, he was
finally sent on his way with a large matronly flea in his ear.

Even so, someone brought me a newspaper a few days
later. 'Syd Little in Heart Attack Scare', read the headlines.
'That's it then,' I thought. 'The career's over.' I looked across
to a ward full of ailing men and my heart sank further into

the depths. 'Even if I survive this one, no one will book an act with a dodgy heart,' I reasoned with myself.

Between blocks of what seemed to be endless sleep induced by the medication, I continued to reflect on my youth and early musical ambitions. My taste for music must have come from Dad who was a very keen trumpet player. He had played it in the RAF but, due to a split lip, swapped brass for an accordion.

In my parents' front room was an old piano and, along with my brother's drum kit and my guitar, it soon became our first musical playroom. Music was a big part of my life as a teenager in the 1950s and the Locarno Dance Hall was a regular haunt. It was at a time when teenagers started to get their own identity with the birth of rock 'n' roll. One of the disc jockeys at the Locarno was a very young Jimmy Saville, who was one of the forerunners of what was to become disco.

Eddie had been one of a regular group of guys I met down there each weekend, but we viewed each other with some disdain. I think we were actually scared of each other because he looked pretty tough to me and the first time he saw me in my crew cut and demob suit he thought I was pretty hard-looking, too. His gang and my gang were rivals and we could easily have starred in a version of *West Side Story*.

After several weeks, we eventually got talking, found some shared interests and I agreed to let him join me in my make-shift recording studio in my front room at home. As I was into all the new technology of the day, I had saved up my lowly decorator's wages and bought a Vox C-30. This was the type of amplifier that the Beatles owned, so, when we all got together to rehearse it sounded good. We all stood there in my front room feeling like we were the bees knees.

An old reel-to-reel tape machine recorded our first attempts and I wish I could get hold of one today. The machine that is, not the recording! Who can imagine what sort of noise we made as we practised all the songs of the day? I bet we sounded terrible, but not as bad as when I started playing guitar. In fact my own guitar playing was so awful, my family often sent me to the downstairs loo whenever I wanted to practise. It was probably while sitting in the smallest room in the house that an ambition to perform on stage was born. Interestingly enough, music was to remain a central part of Little and Large's success and, in another quite amazing way, was to bring me full circle in the years ahead.

'We've got the results of your tests, Mr Little.'

My thoughts snapped back to reality once more as I looked up to see the white-coated physician standing over me, leafing through a set of papers clipped together in a worn-out brown file. Over the last few days, I had been plugged in to various instruments that would surely give some indication as to the condition of my heart.

'So what's happening?' I said, wondering if I really wanted to hear what he had to say.

'Well, it seems that you are on the mend,' he said abruptly. 'We cleared the blood clot. We shall still have to keep an eye on you, but I think we caught you just in time.' He gave a quick smile and walked away.

I was left with a whole mixture of new emotions that now seemed to boil up like bubbles from a Jacuzzi somewhere deep down inside. The biggest bubble of all was an enormous sense of being mightily glad to be alive, and it seemed that I had a good chance of remaining that way.

'Six weeks off?!' our agent had shouted back at me down the phone. I had told him that I was now back at home but had to take things easy for a while. He was beside himself. With the thought of all those lost bookings for one of his best-earning acts, I could well appreciate why. Little and Large had been the subject of *This is Your Life* just a few weeks previously and he was understandably keen to follow this highlight with as much work as possible.

For the moment, however, my thoughts were firmly focused on enjoying being back home and getting better. The career could wait and, as I had only ever considered our success to be a gift rather than a right, letting go was easy.

We lived in a nice house in Torquay, Devon, and, for once, I was able to appreciate the seaside for its harbour and its boats and soak up the holiday atmosphere rather than be diving in and out of its theatres and clubs. Life suddenly seemed to go more slowly and, with each day, I grew physically stronger.

Living in Torquay meant that I was being looked after at Torbay General Hospital and, as far as I was concerned, they had done a tremendous job of saving my life. What happened next was down to me. Equally, the doctor's comments that they should keep a close eye on me soon turned into the reality of regular hospital visits, tests and chats with my GP.

The running machine was to be my first step towards discovering just how damaged my heart had actually been and what the longer-term effects were likely to be. Standing on the moving rubber mat with wires attached to my back, arms and nipples, I started to smile as thoughts of Norman Wisdom and his comic films sprang to mind. My eagerness to revive my comedy instinct got the better of me when I tried to crack a joke at the operator twiddling the knobs of the machine I was connected to. This was a sure sign that I was getting better!

'Don't let those electrical impulses be sent the wrong way or it'll make more than the hair on my head stand up!'

The response was a firm rebuke to concentrate on what I was about to do. The uncomfortable lack of laughter instantly took my thoughts back to some of the more dismal working men's clubs where Eddie and I performed 20 years ago and struggled to get laughs.

When the ground beneath my feet began to move, I walked with it, step by step.

'Just keep walking as the mat moves forward,' instructed the deadpan voice.

I started off at a slow walking pace, but it gradually increased until it felt like I was training for a marathon. My heart was starting to pump loudly and the bleep-bleep of the machine got faster and louder. Despite the strain on my muscles and heart, I wasn't scared because I was in hospital already, secure in the knowledge that the paramedics were not far away and a defribulator was hanging on the wall right in front of me!

After ten minutes of walking for what seemed to be the equivalent of going up and down the Yorkshire hills for hours, the treadmill began to slow down and eventually stopped. A brief smile from the operator confirmed that my trial had shown some measure of success, but now it was down to the doctor to interpret the results.

As I walked into his room, I was holding my breath in nervous anticipation.

'Take a seat, Mr Little,' he beckoned without looking away from the folds of paper in front of him.

I sat in silence and heard my deep breathing play alongside the steady beat of my heart as if they were both in discussion with the heart specialist. After a while, he looked up, slightly baffled.

'Your heart seems to be fine,' he said. 'I can't see any obvious damage at all.'

I looked at him blankly. He said that, apparently, the drugs they had given me in A&E had blown the blockage in my artery away in one go. It was considered that I was very lucky indeed.

The relief on my face must have been quite a picture because his serious manner gave way to a gentle smile before he went on to a more solemn conversation.

'No smoking. Five portions of fruit a day. Try the occasional glass of red wine.'

As Mum and Dad had smoked like chimneys, our little corporation house always stank of smoke, so my brother, sister and I were put off the habit right from the start. This bit of advice wasn't going to be a problem. Also, I'd always enjoyed fruit at home, but the best news was the wine. I'm a sucker for red wine and even today I can enjoy a bottle on my own after a show. Now, with the thought that it might be doing me some good, it is even more of a pleasure!

I beamed at the good doctor, but he stayed serious.

'We shall still need to monitor the situation, of course, and further checks are needed,' he said. 'An angiogram will be best.'

It was not until many months later that I returned to hospital, ready for this delicate procedure. We had moved home during this time, from Torquay to Fleetwood. It seemed that, while living in Devon, all the work was up north. This seemed to suggest that we should move to be nearer to work, but, as soon as we moved, I was constantly travelling down south again. To cap it all, we even ended up doing a series of dates back in good old Torquay. The best place to live for our business was perhaps the Midlands, I mused. Then I'd probably be offered a season in Corfu, so I'd never win.

'You do realize the risks involved?' asked a concerned-looking specialist when I arrived at Blackpool General Hospital. 'It's a dangerous procedure that could cause the heart to stop if anything goes wrong.'

'Yes, that's fine. The doctor has explained it all to me,' I answered, with little real confidence.

I lay on the bed and waited as the local anaesthetic began to paralyze the lower part of my body.

'We are going to fill your body with a fluid that will help us to see inside your heart. It'll make you feel like you want to go to the toilet,' explained the specialist.

Moments after feeling the needle penetrate, there was a whoosh inside me that made me feel like I was going to burst.

Once the lubrication was administered, the specialist entered the room for the next step of the process. I turned to look at the overhead monitor as the tiny camera was inserted into my groin and pushed up through the arteries and on into my heart. If I hadn't known what I was seeing, I would have been certain that the picture I could see on the screen was the driver's view of a tube train speeding along the different tunnels of an underground rail system. Whether it was the Bakerloo Line, or with the bloated way I was feeling, the Waterloo Line, I couldn't decide – it was just the strangest experience altogether.

'Well, Mr Little,' said the doctor after a journey of about 15 minutes, 'I really can't see any problems. Your heart seems to have repaired itself.'

The doctor signed me off then and there and, as I sat pondering for a while waiting for Sheree to come and take me home, I realized just how lucky I had been. God had answered my prayers, but not in the way I had expected. I had accepted the fact that I should be dead by now, but he had decided that I was still going to be around to look after my family and I would get to see Dominic grow up after all.

While I was sitting there, I was spotted by a sweet Irish couple who rushed over to me and asked for an autograph. I couldn't have been more delighted. Despite the fact that the piece of paper they handed to me to write on was an invitation to a prenatal class, it felt that, after all I had been through, this was the most significant autograph I had ever written.

Then another man came up to me.

'Hi, Syd!'

Something inside caused me to think that this man was significant in some odd way.

'I was in the next bed to you in hospital,' he bellowed.

He had been the person in the centre of the medical drama when I had awoken that night to hear someone being resuscitated.

'Well, it's really nice to meet you,' I smiled. 'I thought you were dead!'

Meeting the man I thought had passed away in the bed next to me seemed like an extra miracle on top of me surviving against the odds. It was like a heavenly confirmation that there was indeed a future in store for me. I went home with a new skip in my step and a joyful realization that God hadn't quite finished with me yet.

2

CHANGING NAMES

I have never been able to handle confrontation. I suppose it's not surprising how much I fear a quarrel given my childhood. I always thought I had a good time as a kid and I felt loved and accepted like any normal family should. The only problem was Mum and Dad's quarrels. I often lay in bed at night and could hear them arguing away. It wasn't a nice experience, but I never thought that it was anything to be really worried about. The funny thing was that I could never hear Mum's voice. Her mellow tones just weren't equal to Dad's hollering, particularly when he was a little worse for wear having been down at the Sale Hotel Public House.

One night, their rowing must have been particularly bad because, when I woke up in the morning, I found our next-door neighbour, Mrs Mare, in our house. Apparently Mum had been so angry that she had stormed out of the house and, having heard the all-night row, Mrs Mare stepped in to help us kids get dressed.

Perhaps it was the fact that Dad got bored with his work easily that caused him to swap jobs so many times. Even as a trained electrician, he changed to working as a labourer, then builder, bricklayer and even a steeplejack. The insecurity and lack of decent income that this resulted in had obviously been at the root of all the arguing and it had all come to a head that night for Mum and she had suddenly upped and left. Although we put a brave face on it, it was a very scary time for me and my brother and sister. We were given no real explanation of what was going on, where Mum was or when she was coming back. We all wondered if we would ever see her again. Dad did his best, but it was Mrs Mare who took over the household reins until Mum eventually arrived back home the next day. Then she carried on as if nothing had happened and we were all too scared to ask any questions.

I suppose what it taught me was that arguments can cause disasters and these can be avoided by staying quiet. Confrontation could lead to people walking out on me. Not a good nor helpful lesson, but I went into life trying to avoid it nonetheless. I was always a bit gullible, too. I was the one who seemed to act as the scapegoat for everyone else. On one occasion, I went camping in the Lake District with my mate Fred and a gang of others from our neighbourhood and the weekend finished in a way that I didn't expect. Fred and I were the last to pack up our tents and, as we left the field, the farmer came up and asked for the collection of half-crowns that were owed to him.

'That'll be three pounds and sixpence,' he said gruffly.

Apparently all the guys who left before us had told him that I would settle the bill for everybody.

'We've only got the money to pay for ourselves,' we said shakily as Fred and I tried to stand our ground and refuse to pay for the others. If I had had the spare cash on me, I'm sure I would have paid up, just to save the situation. As it was, the farmer glared at us for a few moments then jumped on to his tractor and chased after our mates, who had long since gone. Needless to say, he didn't catch them, but when Fred and I arrived at the ferry to take us across the lake back home, there were a lot of white faces and wide eyes looking straight at me.

'Hey, Syd, we need your guitar!' they said when I got on board. They seemed suspiciously overly pleased to see me. Although my guitar was something that travelled with me wherever I went, I still thought it was a funny time to ask me to play. I soon realized that they had other ideas.

As the ferry took off for its short run across the lake, they each handed me a camping knife until I had half a dozen and told me that I had to hide them inside my guitar. They ignored the puzzled look on my face and my eager questions, only anxious to see the job done. I just managed to fit all the knives into the small circular hole when the boat arrived at the other side and a couple of policemen jumped on board, grabbed the lads and started to frisk them. Somehow, the farmer had passed on a message to say that he had been threatened at knifepoint by the lads and the police had taken him at his word. He'd got his own back. Now here was I, shaking in my shoes, walking off the ferry, trying to look all innocent and calm, pretending that I had nothing to do with the lads, but with a guitar full of lethal weapons. The lads got a two-year ban from the Lake District as a result of their behaviour towards the farmer, but it's not the first time my guitar came in handy, as you will see later.

After a day potholing we used to meet in a pub called the Lord Nelson in Didsbury. When I was leading a singalong, Eddie suddenly got up beside me on the little wobbly stage to do an impression of Gene Vincent, of 'Be Bop a Lula' fame. Eddie picked up a mop to use as a mic stand, then slipped on some beer, went sliding across the platform and down on to the floor, breaking the mop in two. The whole place was in hysterics because it looked so funny and, as Eddie handled it all so well, everybody thought it was part of an act.

Above the laughter rose a very agitated voice. The landlady was incensed.

'That's my b****y mop you've busted there, lad. You'll have to pay for it you know!'

With her mop now in pieces, we didn't want to upset her any more, so we all had a quick whip-round for a new one, but the beginnings of Little and Large had been born.

We enjoyed ourselves so much that night and had our audience laughing so easily, that we soon repeated the whole act at every opportunity we had, mostly at weekends, at parties, at work dos and the pub. The antics we got up to on stage together lasted longer and longer and Eddie started to specialize in doing impressions and funny voices. As our bit of fun caught on, we received more and more invitations from local pubs and, eventually, had our first night's paid work.

I was already being paid to sing regularly at several clubs in the area. In one of these, the landlady Mrs Allcock had a habit of pulling her double-barrelled shotgun out of a cupboard when it was closing time in order to encourage everyone to get out more quickly. It was never loaded and I think it was a bit of a gimmick, but it certainly did the trick. Hers must have been the quickest emptying pub in history! I specialized in comedy numbers such as 'My Old Man's a Dustman' and 'What a Picture' or 'Little White Bull'. Three pounds a night was the kind of extra pocket money an adolescent boy like me eagerly desired to take the girls out. Not that I had much success at that – my National Health glasses and the only grey suit I had that I wore each time made me look like I had just come out of prison!

I took my first girl home from the Navigation Pub. She was blonde, 16 and had never been kissed. At least that's what she told me! I thought I had won the star prize as she offered to take me home with her. After a short train ride, during which we tried to fit in as many kisses as possible, I was still gulping for air when she pulled me off the train at her station. She took me straight to the guinnell – an alleyway at the back of her house – and there the snogging continued. I wondered where all this was going to lead to and, to be honest, we were all so ignorant about sex in those days, I really hadn't a clue.

All of a sudden she stood back from me and said,

'Se ya then!'

I was still leaning against the wall when she upped and left as if she had been frightened off by a ghost. I dusted myself down and decided that if that was what romance was all about, I would rather stick to my guitar. Surely that would never walk out on me!

It was at the Timperley Trade and Labour Club that Eddie asked if he could come on stage with me once more. We had already rehearsed songs such as 'Rubber Ball' and Eddie's Cliff Richard impressions, so we were pretty confident. The act was the best we had ever been. The applause echoed around the buildings as we went off stage at the end and the concert secretary, who was responsible for making the bookings, immediately asked us back as a double act for the grand sum of £6. Agreeing to split this sum down the middle, I ended up with the same amount that I had been paid as a solo performer, but I knew that the act we had unwittingly created was something new and different.

The only thing we needed now was a proper name. We formulated our first stage name by combining our surnames. I was Cyril Mead and Eddie was Edward McGuiness. The problem was that, when we were announced as 'Mead and McGuiness', the audience thought we were a brewery! We soon became simply 'Syd and Eddie'. Not very inspiring, I know, but it was all we could think of at the time.

We ticked over with one or two gigs a week, but one day we had a big falling out over something and I told Eddie that I didn't want to work with him any more. I had really had enough of this sort of stress.

The next day, back at home, Dad shouted upstairs to me.

'Cyril! Eddie's at the door.'

I came down to see a very sheepish-looking human being huddled in the doorway.

'I'm really sorry, Syd,' he said.

I gave him my hand, we shook and carried on.

We had plenty of arguments, but you could count on one hand the big rows. Eddie said I was the easygoing one and the one that always gave in. The thing we discovered was that when we had one of these rare bust-ups and then had to go on stage to get laughs, we just couldn't look each other in the eye. It definitely affected our act, and we somehow knew the audience could feel that something wasn't right between us. We had to get that personal contact back quickly or we knew we couldn't have gone on.

The number of bookings increased and word soon got round that we were a good – and probably very cheap – act. One gig at the weekend soon became two, then three, then we worked weekdays, travelling further and further each time. When I found that I could earn more money doing the act than my proper job as a painter and decorator, I agreed with Eddie that we should turn professional. I got £50 a week doing the act rather than 2 shillings and sixpence. It was one of the most exciting periods of my life – I even bought my first car, an Austin 1100.

My brother David was our roadie at the time, though the funny thing was that he couldn't drive! We were the butt of many of the other acts' jokes when they realized that.

We started to work further afield, away from Manchester, and frequently in the North East of England. We stayed in pro-digs – bed and breakfasts that accommodated acts working in the local venues. The great thing about our change of job and the beauty of these places was that we didn't have to get up till midday for breakfast, and there was always a supper waiting for us in the oven when we got back in the early hours of the next morning. All this at the cost of £9 a week. What a bargain!

The odd thing is that we were never very close friends off stage. We hardly spent any time together socially – it was as if our relationship was almost purely based on the act. Eddie was starting to play golf and follow his beloved Manchester

City FC, but I was interested in model making and music. On stage, we sparkled and the chemistry worked, but off stage, apart from the extensive travelling we started to do together, we often went our separate ways.

Why did the chemistry work on stage? I've no idea. It's like asking what makes a hit record. If we knew the answer to that we'd all be millionaires.

People always ask me if it was hardgoing in the early days of the act, but I always say 'no' because we really didn't know any better. We only had the suits we stood up in. We did our spot as best we could, then went to the bar for a drink and never imagined that it would go any further. It was as simple as that. There was no ambition to become household names, no drive to become rich, no illusions of grandeur. We just accepted what we had and never entertained any fantasies about becoming big stars. That was well out of our league anyway – so we thought.

We didn't even wear make-up on stage. We hadn't met anyone from the real side of showbusiness, in working theatres rather than pubs and clubs, and had no idea that it was this that made them look so good on stage and television. When we had rushed round to stage doors to see our musical and comedy heroes coming out, we hadn't realized that they had washed it all off. We considered any bloke wearing make-up and powder was to be avoided at all costs!

It wasn't until we worked with an act called Miki and Griff at the Yew Tree Pub in Manchester that we began to realize something was missing from the visual side of our act. As we had progressed in our career from working men's clubs to venues with proper stage facilities, we hadn't realized that we looked pale and ill under the glare of the lights.

Miki and Griff were famous for a number of pop hits, including 'Puff the Magic Dragon' and 'Little Bitty Tear' and, as we sat talking to them backstage one day, they unpacked a whole load of jars, sponges, creams and eyeliners from their bags and started to get made up. Even Griff, who sported a huge moustache, started to wipe a tan-coloured cream over his face and put two little red dots in the corners of his eyes as he carried on chatting nonchalantly. Eddie and I threw a sideways glance at each other with wide eyes and a worried smile until Miki turned to us and said,

'Well, nearly time to start. Are you not making up, boys?'

'Of course!' said I, lying in the most convincing way I could manage.

I really didn't know what I had said or what I had meant, but Eddie and I went out on stage that night feeling rather naked. Deciding next day to be properly professional, I went to the local fancy dress shop and, among all the ballet dresses and clowns outfits, asked for what I thought was the make-up I needed. When they asked me what shade I wanted I just said 'brown, please'!

It was Max Factor 28, bunged on with some water and a sponge, and it's still basically the same today. I had a bit of a try-out at home and anxiously applied the wet mixture to my face, hoping that no one would turn up unexpectedly while I was in the process of applying it. It all looked fine to me, but when I repeated the process in the club that night, Eddie burst into fits of laughter.

'Are you doing a minstrels show?' he said mockingly.

When I looked in the mirror at my tanned face and huge glasses, it looked as if I had just come back from a year in Barbados. To make matters worse, when I glanced down at my hands, they looked as though I was wearing white gloves compared with the heavy brown on my face. There wasn't time to change anything before we were on stage and I felt very odd all the way through. I'm sure the audience thought I was going to break into 'Swanee' at any moment.

Another thing we were not used to were rooms to change in. We followed a singer into the club one night only to hear him say to the man backstage,

'Where's the dressing room, mate?'

'What's a dressing room?' we said to each other in bafflement. We were many years away from beautiful backstage suites with endless drinks on the house and make-up artists and hairdressers waiting to meet our every whim.

'Down the end of the corridor, turn left,' said the stage manager. 'Syd and Eddie, you're in number four, down the stairs and turn right.'

Following his directions, we found a room with our name on the door and seats and tables inside. We thought we had just won the pools. Par for the course up until now was to change in the cellar along with the barrels. We tried to look our best despite the circumstances, but always smelt of beer. Bernard Manning's Embassy Club in Manchester was a fine example of how used we had got to roughing it off stage. As I say in my act today, '. . . it was that rough, Kate Adie was on the door and there was a pig on the bar as an air freshener!' We were booked to do three clubs a night, seven nights a week, but Bernard's was the most unusual because it looked like we were performing in a railway tunnel. The venue was very long, with an arched ceiling. The bar was on one side of the wall and the only door was at the back of the club. Once inside, you were trapped until it was time to leave. This meant that if any of the performers were taken short, it was a major problem because there was simply nowhere to 'go'.

Bernard had his own way of dealing with this though.

'Hold that door!' he bellowed at me one night.

'Sorry, Bernard?' I was totally confused.

'Hold that bl***ing door,' he repeated, gesturing towards a cupboard. I opened it and could see a large hole in the floor, at which point Bernard made arrangements to relieve himself. I couldn't believe what I was seeing.

The other problem with having the door at the back was that we had to fight our way through the crowd to get backstage and afterwards fight our way back out through the same crowd of people who had just watched us perform. This was fine so long as the act had gone down well. A few handshakes and a 'Good on ya boys' was always welcome as we left. If, however, our act had not gone so well, perhaps due to bad timing or the wrong kind of jokes for the wrong kind of audience, it was a totally different matter. Many were the times we battled our way through an angry audience who felt that they had been cheated in some way. Even Bernard, who was the show's compere, spotted us ploughing our way back through the crowd one night and shouted, 'Absolute rubbish!' across the PA as we tried to scurry out. 'Look at 'em both,' he said. 'One's like a Watney's red barrel and the other's like a drainpipe. In fact, if Syd turned sideways and stuck out his tongue, he'd look like a zip!' 'Let's hope you're better tomorrow . . . if we're lucky!' was ringing in our ears as we finally burst though the back door and out into the midnight air. The evening was a bad one, but at least Eddie was now the proud owner of a quick-fire gag about my size that he then used for the rest of our career!

By this time, we were being invited back to so many clubs and pubs around Manchester that we both agreed that the act needed to change to keep it fresh. We also still needed a proper stage name. Being known locally as Syd and Eddie was fine, but when we started to get bookings further afield, the names just didn't seem to work. It all came to a head one night when we were working in a club in Lewes near Brighton. The booker, a man named Joe Collins – Joan Collins' father – was acting as our agent in the south.

We went to see Joe in his posh flat in London's Marylebone. As we walked into the room, with its thick-pile carpet, we looked at the wall, which was covered with pictures of all the big stars of the day. Among all these were pictures of Joan Collins and Anthony Newley, who were married at the time, and we wondered if we would be on his wall one day, too.

Joe sat us down and started to give us a professional pep talk. It wasn't good enough to be an exciting up-and-coming act, he explained, we needed a good name, too. He said that introducing an act with names like Fred and Charlie just wasn't exciting enough for anyone who didn't know us.

'Please welcome Fred and Charlie . . .' he shouted out as an example and we could immediately see what he meant. It sounded like an anti-climax.

'Now, the guy at Lewes wants to book you again,' he went on. 'But not as Syd and Eddie. I'm afraid you will have to come up with a better name.'

The next day, Eddie went to a second-hand shop, bought an old typewriter and sat up all the next night typing out suggestions. In the morning, a very sleepy Eddie handed me the long list and there, right in the middle, was the name Little and Large. There was no question. This was ideal and we adopted it from that day on.

We went back to Joe with the new name and he loved it. Two years later, we went back to see him in his flat. We noticed that the pictures of Joan Collins and Anthony Newley had been removed, because they had now divorced, and hoped that our association with Joe and the London showbiz scene would not go the same way.

After finding a new name, we turned our attention to creating new material. It's always difficult to change tried and trusted routines for something fresh and the temptation is to stick with what you know works best. Even so, we batted out our own ideas. Whenever I came up with a suggestion, it never seemed good enough for Eddie. It seemed as if his ideas were always fully embraced, though, and I just gave in again – always the one to avoid confrontation.

What is strange about all this is that when most people look at a double act, they see how well they behave on stage together and imagine it's like that all the time. For example, it always amazed me how people really did believe Cannon and Ball's continuous gag that they lived in a caravan together when, in fact, they demanded separate dressing rooms at opposite ends of the theatre and didn't even talk to each other for five years at the height of their fame. Even I don't know how they managed to continue so professionally without the audience ever knowing.

It's this kind of tension between two people that actually makes the comedy fireworks ignite. A guitar with loose strings won't play properly, but tightening them enables accurate and clear notes to be played and so it is with comedy. The tension between an audience and a comedian is vital and the tension between two halves of a double act even more so.

There were other double acts that were the same, and I would watch them have fights before going on stage, do the act, come off and continue the scrap. Those who didn't have this type of antagonistic relationship were often the ones who didn't last. Gentle and Giant spring to mind. They were a couple of nice guys who sadly never got beyond the club circuit. Mind you, it could have been that they were too similar to Little and Large. It always hurts when an original routine of yours is used by someone else. Another double act who continue to work today still use our original guitar routine!

Although I appreciated the need for pressure between Eddie and I to make the act work, for me, it was sometimes the wrong sort of pressure.

I continued to keep my head down as much as possible, and often felt stupid that I had not stood up for myself more often. Eddie never suggested this, but I think that had I done so, the act would never have survived and what a shame that would have been. What drove me on was the fact that I was really beginning to enjoy the showbiz lifestyle alongside the challenge of improving the act and the quality of the bookings.

In 1964, we had our first ever theatre date, but it was a disaster. It was in Blackpool – the Mecca of showbusiness. 'One more step on from this and we shall be at the London Palladium,' we joked as we walked along the promenade. However, little did we know when we arrived at the Queen's Theatre that we were about to endure a very painful experience, one that was to change the shape of our act for good.

The show was all put together at the last minute because a play called *Man in the Moon* hadn't been as successful as expected and was to finish its run early. We were to be part of a new run of variety with Sabrina, the sex symbol of the day, topping the bill. Pop star Pat O'Hare and the Jones Boys, four men who did impressions, also starred. We were the comic double act. We were asked not to forget to bring our music, but, the fact was, we had no real music.

'I shall need full orchestral parts,' said the musical director.

Up until then, we had only needed parts for bass, piano and drums, because that's all the clubs needed. Where on earth were we to get 'dots' for trumpet, trombone, percussion . . . ? The list went on and on.

We gave a friend of ours the piano parts and were thrilled when he handed us back armfuls of sheet music a few days later. Neither of us could read music, but it all looked good enough to us.

'Well, that was simple enough,' I said to Eddie.

It had cost us a fortune – more than we were going to earn for the week – but having proper parts now armed us with the confidence we needed to be real theatre entertainers, rather than just a run-of-the-mill club act.

When we got to the theatre later that week, we rushed on to the stage like two excited little boys and proudly put the pile of papers down at the front under the nose of the musical director. Someone had told us that when you arrive at a theatre band call, the first act to put their parts on the edge of the stage is rehearsed first. However, this person neglected to mention that there is also such a thing as a pecking order! The long cold stare that resulted from the musical director sent a shiver down my spine.

'Miss Sabrina will be first,' he announced, in a very flat, formal voice.

The lady herself arrived and we offered a weak and slightly embarrassed smile. When Sabrina was happy with the sound and tempo of her music and our faces had resumed their normal colour, the musical director reached out and seemed slightly reluctant to pick up the huge pile of music in front of him. As he began to hand the parts out among his orchestra, I couldn't help thinking that the look on his face said it all – 'If these two guys are comedians, why have they got so much music?'

His confusion soon turned to complete bewilderment when he struck up the orchestra for our entrance music and what came out seemed like three or four different tunes all at the same time. It was a complete cacophony of noise that, with a flick of his baton and a frown on his face, stopped as abruptly as it had started.

'I've got no words on my part!' shouted the trumpet player.

'This doesn't make any sense!' cried the guitarist.

'Can you explain how this bridge works?' yelled the pianist.

As neither Eddie nor I could read music, the best we could do was hum how it should go. We did short bursts of songs from pop singers like Freddie and the Dreamers and Mick Jagger in those days, so it took ages to explain how it all linked musically. To make matters worse, every time we sorted out a song, a well-dressed man appeared on stage from somewhere in the wings and said,

'Sorry lads, you can't do that. The Jones Boys do Mick Jagger.'

'Sorry lads, you can't do that. The Jones Boys do Freddie and the Dreamers.'

Slowly we saw our act going out the window. Two hours and much humming later, we finally emerged triumphant, but with an exhausted set of musicians and an angry gang of other acts who hadn't been able to get a band call for themselves.

Even though the biggest parts of our act were now missing, we went on stage and did two performances that night with a very good response from the audience. We were mighty relieved, but made up our minds that our band parts would always be properly written by a professional from that day onwards.

After the show, we were asked to pop up and see the theatre manager. Expecting hearty congratulations, we marched into his office with beaming smiles and were really shocked when he announced in his broad Scottish accent,

'Sorry lads, but we were told you were patter comedians. You do too much music and we've a lot of music on the show already. I shall have to pay you off.'

We walked out of his room stunned and sat in silence all the way back to Manchester, which was broken only by the occasional whimper from Eddie who had tears running down his face.

It was one of the turning points for the act, though, because the next day we met up to discuss how we could avoid such a disaster again, perhaps by having more stand-up material. So we made up our minds to put more patter and less music in the act and it has remained so to this day.

Worse disasters were to come in the years of our TV shows, but these all began with an appearance on the talent show *Opportunity Knocks*, which led to our television career taking off. Little did we know that the real show had only just begun.

3

OPPORTUNITY KNOCKS

Mavis was only 16 when we first met. She was my sister Linda's best friend, a lovely looking girl and someone I became very fond of. I had no intention of making it a serious relationship, though, particularly as I knew that she, like most, found it hard to cope with the strange lifestyle of the entertainer in which I would be there one minute and gone the next. When Eddie and I got our first summer season in Jersey, she came too and arranged for her job in a Mansfield shoe shop to be transferred to one on Jersey. We spent the summer in the same low-budget lodgings with leaky taps and greasy tablecloths with our respective girls because Eddie had married Sandra, his first wife, by this time. The girls didn't get on and it was a bit of a bumpy ride, particularly when we discovered that Mavis was pregnant.

At the end of the season, I decided that I should do the honourable thing and marry Mavis, so I did. We had the celebration at St Michael's and All Angels, my childhood church, and Paul was born a few months later.

Sadly, parenthood and showbiz never seemed to mix. I was working at a club in Sunderland when I got a telephone call from Mavis' mother to tell me that Paul had been born. I had been on tenterhooks all week because I knew the baby was due, but I hadn't got a clue where I would be on the big day. 'I hope it waits until I get home for my day off,' I had said to Eddie. Every day that went by I had wondered if I would get a call and, in the days before mobile telephones, I had to give Mavis a long list of contact numbers for all the clubs we were appearing at. Sometimes there were three different clubs a night.

They were pretty rough places and we soon learnt that to get the audience's attention you had to hit them hard with very quick, noisy and punchy routines right from the beginning. Each spot had to last half an hour as we were on between bingo sessions. Over the years, the clubs had become more demanding, wanting anything up to four spots a night to make sure their audiences stayed near to the bar as long as possible. One day, we decided that doing what amounted to two hours with the same audience was too much. It wasn't time that was the problem, but the fact that each time we went on we were trying to come up with better and better material, which was extremely difficult to achieve, even for the biggest stars of the day. Eventually, we would only agree to two spots in one place and the other entertainers started to follow suit. Some of the clubs remained indignant, though. The concert chairman, known as the con. sec., would always try to make us do more than we agreed. One chairman was so annoyed at our resistance to doing more spots that he tried to get his own back when he introduced us.

'Well we've got Little and Large here tonight, but they'll only do two spots for us 'cos they've got to be away by 'alf past ten to go to another club so's they get another 25 quid.'

That was our introduction. We bounced on stage and instantly 'died' in front of 200 miners who had to spend a whole week down the pit in order to earn the same amount of money.

A rhyme I found written on the backstage wall of a working men's club sums it all up:

You found the club, arrived on time,
Con. sec. greets you and all is fine.
Dressing room next to stage, bingo goes on for an
   age.
You change your suit, sort out your dots.
Con. sec. says, 'I want five spots'.

'They like old ballads here, nothing mod.
I was first in't north to book Ken Dodd.
Here's our duo, best in't land,
Drummer played in colliery band.
Our organist is Tommy Speed,
Real good player but cannot read.'

Bingo's finished, half audience has gone,
Ready lads, I'll put thee on.
'Give order now for Syd and Eddie,
Pies and pasties now on sale,
Get them while you're ready.'

You try your best, the mic is bad,
The backing is the worst we've had.
The audience applaud them rapturously,
Your turn, more ballads you try in vain,
Con. sec. says, 'Don't go on again.
They don't like you lads, your style is wrong,
You only know one kind of song.'

'All of them old ballads, nothing mod.
I was first in't north to book Ken Dodd.'
You're driving home, feeling sad,
But can things really be that bad?
You've got showbusiness in your bones
And let's face it, some folks don't like Tom Jones.

When I got the phone call from Mavis' mother to tell me that Paul had been born, I had already performed in three clubs that night. The roads were not as good as they are today and, with the heavy snow that was falling, it took me nearly three hours to get to Sale, near Manchester. I arrived at three in the morning and collapsed into bed. Visiting Mavis at the hospital the next morning, I gave newborn Paul a quick hug, then got back on the road to get to the next night's set of gigs. New fatherhood wasn't meant to be like this – for me it was a fleeting moment. Then, when Donna was born, 18 months later in October 1969, it seemed like I spent even less time at home. I carried the guilt of being an absent father for many years afterwards.

The amount of travelling we did at this time was horrendous and, in 1969, Eddie and I had played at the Hartlepool Working Men's club and were driving along the A19 through Sunderland to get to Newcastle. In the darkness I noticed a car speeding along a side road and, for some reason, I knew that he wasn't going to stop at the junction. In fact, he headed straight for us and I tried to brake, but it was too late. There was an almighty crunch as the car ploughed into the side of us and, the next thing I knew, two men were standing me up against a wall trying to revive me. I heard someone shout something about it all going to catch fire and saw Eddie, frantically trying to get our PA system out of the boot of the car.

It wasn't long before the ambulance came and took me to Sunderland General Hospital, where I stayed for the next few days. I was fortunate that, despite the seriousness of the accident, I had not broken anything and just needed a few stitches in my knees and one eyelid. When I came out on crutches a few days later, it seemed as if every bone in my body ached. Eddie came out unscathed, as did our precious PA system – now essential for our gigs. We were told by the car recovery garage how lucky we were to be alive.

Eddie played at many gigs we had been booked to do for the rest of the week and, the following Sunday, came and sat on the edge of my bed at home. He pulled the money he had earned that week out of his pocket and handed me half. It was a generous act that I have never forgotten.

It was in 1971 that we started working with a new agent called Major Brian Hart, who also managed the pop group Paper Lace, of 'Billy Don't Be a Hero' fame. The Major had spotted us in a club and took us on. He was quite a character and would drive round in a Rolls-Royce, with gold chains dripping from his neck and wrists – not the conventional army type! He took us the next step up in the business, but we were still very much at the learning stage.

The Major had dreams of making us television stars and wanted us to audition for the talent contest famously presented by Hughie Green, but, because Eddie and I had already been going a number of years, we felt that this was a bit below us. Major Hart agreed and so, instead, turned his attentions towards Royston Mayoh, the programme's producer and talent scout. He sent him letters, messages and constantly telephoned him, badgering Roy to come and see this great 'new' double act. Eventually, after weeks of this consistent onslaught from the Major, Roy came to see us at the Wookey Hollow Club in Liverpool. He brought three of his colleagues with him so that, under the rules of the TV show, it could be deemed an official audition.

We must have passed because Roy was thrilled at what he saw and pleased with how well the comic chemistry worked on stage for us and travelled out into the howling audience. Only time would tell if our success in a live venue could be effectively transferred to the medium of television, but it was certainly worth a try and we decided that we had nothing to lose.

Hughie Green, the show's presenter, was probably the first popular star of early British television and his talent show went on to launch the careers of many great acts, such as Les Dawson, Pam Ayres and Max Boyce. Mr Muscles, Bobby Crush and Freddie Starr were also discovered by the show. Hughie Green had been a child film star and his grandfather was the famous music hall comic Harry Tate so he knew about the business. We had heard stories about Hughie being difficult to work with but when we met him he seemed very pleasant and a true professional.

When we faced the cameras and the lights, it all seemed to go smoothly and we were amazed when we won. At first, this was in the studio with the infamous 'Clapometer'. Otherwise known as the 'Audience Reaction Monitor', this was a piece of technical wizardry created by the studio's technical department that supposedly measured the studio audience's response as they voted with their applause and cheers for each act. It gave a visual score that ran along the bottom of the television screen. Most people imagined that there was a little man hidden there with a stick and a rubber band moving the dial more in tune with his own personal view than with what the audience thought. This machine was genuine, however, and was specifically developed and used for Hughie Green's *Opportunity Knocks* and was probably the first kind of interactive TV ever seen in the UK.

Once the live programme had ended, it was time for all those at home to vote and the letters and postcards poured in by the thousands, but Eddie and I had no fingernails left by the end of the week as we awaited the results. The following Monday morning, I got a telephone call from the Major.

'You've won,' he said in my ear, so simply it was as if he was just telling me that I had a dentist's appointment coming up. As I put the telephone back on its rest, I was numb with excitement and disbelief. I'm not normally a noisy person, but I shouted out my exhilaration until everyone inside the house and outside it had no doubt as to what was going on.

Eddie and I shared this great news on the telephone with

each other and, a week later, we were back in the studio, hoping to win again, performing another slice of our act in front of the cameras and the studio audience.

I think Hughie liked our act and, although there were rumours that he would often approach winners with a view to becoming their agent and earning a little extra, he never approached us in this way.

Unfortunately the wider audience wasn't as kind to us that week and we got a solemn call from the Major the following Monday to tell us that we were second.

'Never mind,' he went on. 'They still want you because the winner's got laryngitis and they want you to stand in for her!'

It was an amazing coincidence, but as Glynis Fleetwood, the real winner, was about to be propelled into stardom, she had lost her voice. We thought that perhaps it was because she had been singing so loudly all week with joy that there was nothing left of her vocal chords for the big day itself.

So Eddie and I went on in the star spot in her place and, for years afterwards, everybody thought we had won *Opportunity Knocks* more than just once. In fact, we only entered two talent competitions and in both we were beaten by female vocalists singing either the 'Nun's Chorus' or 'The Lord's Prayer'. Perhaps God was trying to say something to us.

We never returned to *Opportunity Knocks*, but we did star in the all winners shows that they occasionally featured. In those days, a talent show covered a whole range of perform-ance skills. It's sad that 'variety' seems to be a dirty word on television these days, as if it's old-fashioned and no one wants it any more. The fact is that the highest earner in live theatre is still the pantomime and what is this but a variety show with a traditional storyline? Whereas today's talent shows, such as *Fame Academy* or *Pop Idol*, just feature singers, there were dancers, jugglers, contortionists, magicians, comedians and even a man who hit his head with a metal tray in time to the music. I believe that the show's popularity must have had a lot to do with all the different acts involved, keeping the programme fresh each week. In my view, the talent competitions these days seem to be more about becoming a celebrity than developing a real talent. So many performers seem to win the show, only to give up a short time later, when they've had enough of their '15 minutes of fame'.

Winning a TV talent contest in the 1970s was no guarantee that you would then become a star. There was no deal ready and waiting for us, we had to carve out any further chances of success ourselves. Even after becoming a weekly champion of *Opportunity Knocks*, it would still take many years before we would finally be offered our first television series, *The Little & Large Show*. Our 'overnight success' actually took 14 years to achieve! We weren't disappointed that the breakthrough took so long, because we didn't really expect it in the first place. We were just happy to let things tick over at a steady pace and enjoy the experience.

We had already begun to make contacts with others in the professional comedy scene, but now that our career was progressing, so were the chances of meeting the bigger stars. Some of these are still my unsung heroes of comedy. Take Norman Collier – better known as the Chicken Man, who struts around with his jacket over his shoulders in the most hilarious way. He is an extremely clever and funny man and so talented that he is very respected by up-and-coming comedians today, too.

We met him first at the Greasborough social club in 1968, where they did what was known as a 'noon and night' on a Sunday. This was a midday show, after which there was lunch, then bingo and the bar ruled before another performance took place in the evening. Norman Collier was top of the bill and Wally Harper – Bobby Ball's uncle – was a comic support act. Wally just couldn't resist heckling Norman all the way through his noon performance, but Norman, being the gentleman that he is, just carried on and gave us good as he got.

'Have a good 'un lads,' he said to us just as we were about to go on, 'keep 'em laughing!' and we've followed his advice ever since.

Another hero of mine was Tommy Cooper.

'Hello Syd. Hello Eddie,' bellowed this huge man with a huge voice, black suit and fez, as we walked down the hallowed corridors backstage at the London Palladium one day. We were so low on the bill that our names were smaller than the printers', yet Tommy knew who we were and took the trouble to introduce himself. Tommy was an extremely funny man and certainly a one-off. He didn't even need to open his mouth and everyone around him would fall about laughing because he was simply naturally funny. With his colossal frame and feet to match, what chance did he ever have of being taken seriously? It must have been really frustrating for him to try to hold a serious conversation. I remember when I first met him in a bar, he was having pain in his legs.

'Aha, my legs are killing me!' he said and we all collapsed into laughter.

Similarly inclined was Les Dawson, who, with his craggy and grave-looking face, would crack jokes one minute and be serious the next in such a way that I never knew which was which.

Charlie Caroli was Britain's greatest clown and when I was invited to his son's wedding in Blackpool, we arrived for the reception at a local hotel and sat down at the beautifully decorated table for the meal. Prawn cocktails were distributed but almost at once Les piped up with, 'This is no good. I don't want these.'

'What's wrong, Les?' I said.

'These prawns. They smell fishy!'

The whole room was in hysterics because Les' timing and delivery was straight out of one of his famous television sketches – yet he was actually being quite serious. He knew that prawns are off if they smell, had them changed and probably saved all his guests from having dreadful stomach upsets.

Charlie Caroli was from an Italian family, but had French relations, too. What he didn't know about slapstick and how to get instant laughs wasn't worth knowing. Charlie used to be a juggling act and appeared in front of the king and queen of Denmark and even Adolf Hitler. Charlie told me that, after his performance for the German dictator, he was presented with a silver cigarette holder, inscribed for him with Adolf Hitler's name inside. When Charlie was back at home and war was declared, he went to the end of the north pier and threw it into the sea. I wonder what this historic memento would be worth now if he had kept it?

Our win on *Opportunity Knocks* produced a number of different proposals about what to do with us on television. We even got to do a pilot sitcom called *Three in a Bed*, but, as we were comics, not actors, it really wasn't the right TV vehicle for us and the whole idea was scrapped.

Another blip in our career was when we appeared as the presenters of the children's show *Crackerjack*. It could have been a great boost for our public profile, but, again, it wasn't right for us. It also made us look as though we were a kid's act. However, it was a long-running show and with it came our first serious money. The format, with its funny sketches, pranks and quizzes, was pretty enduring, but I don't think it worked as well with a double act as it did with solo acts, such as the late great Leslie Crowther or Peter Glaze and the very funny Don Maclean. Michael Aspel and eventually Ed 'Stewpot' Stewart went on to host it over the years.

Elaine Paige would probably like to forget that she was on *Crackerjack* with us, but, there it is, in the television archives.

We used to share a laugh together whenever I met her in the studio because I teased her about smelling of chips. I think that this was due to the fact that, at the time, she lived in a tiny bedsit near a fish and chip shop and the salt and vinegar fragrance seemed to have permeated everything she wore. Whenever I saw her name in lights after that, I always had a sudden urge for a chip butty.

Alongside Elaine on *Crackerjack* was a lovely, sweet girl called Heather. Playing a Cinderella story one week and standing next to Eddie, she burst into tears.

'I'm supposed to be a juvenile lead and here I am in a tattered old dress playing to kids,' she sobbed.

'*You're* worried?' said Eddie, who was standing beside her, dressed as a very plump fairy, complete with blond wig and thick lipstick. 'Just look at me!'

After 13 weeks of recording the Friday night *Crackerjack* show and then dashing up and down the country to fulfil the club bookings, we were pretty shattered and we knew we had to change our strategy.

Perhaps our manager had been a bit short-sighted and thought that *any* TV exposure would be good, but we were being thought of as children's entertainers and this affected our live audiences and the types of people who came to see us. Often we would run out on to the stage to see a whole row of kids when our act, although never blue, wasn't geared towards youngsters. Naturally, our act instantly lost its bite as we tried not to upset them and their parents.

'We'll ask the Major to change all this,' said Eddie.

As he only had contacts in the Midlands, however, the Major introduced us to Michael Grade. It was he who would be responsible for building our career in London and who introduced us to Norman Murray, who became and then remained our sole agent for the next ten years.

During Christmas 1972, I fell in love. The only problem was that I was already married. However, the hectic lifestyle of showbusiness had caused Mavis and I to drift apart and, by the time Eddie and I were starring in a touring panto with DJ 'Diddy' David Hamilton, I hadn't been home for a very long time.

There was never any doubt about my love for my children, but the showbiz way of life was all-enveloping. I was working among people doing the same job, living the same lifestyle with the same problems. It was like being part of another family, while my real family became sidelined.

When Sheree walked into my life, it was more than just a physical attraction. There was something deeper that happened between us. True, she was one of the loveliest dancers I had ever worked with on a show, but it wasn't her long legs that captivated me – it was her eyes. They were the biggest, bluest eyes I had ever seen and I couldn't resist being drawn to her, even though I knew it would cause huge problems back at home.

Now, with standing ovations and everyone around us telling us how great Eddie and I were and what big stars we were destined to be, we threw ourselves into the showbiz scene even more than 100 per cent. There was little time for anything or anyone else and my marriage to Mavis had no hope of survival.

By contrast, I was seeing Sheree every day and, whenever we could, we would pop over and take Paul and Donna out for a day. They were three and five by this time and Sheree took the situation in her stride. A favourite activity was roller skating at the Nevada rink in Bolton, but I could never keep on my feet. The worst bit was when we would go to Smithills afterwards and I would find it hard sitting down because of all the bruises on my bottom. After a steak and kidney pie and chips, followed by apple pie and custard, we would deliver the children back home to Mavis, who was always pleased to see us.

Despite everything, Mavis was a good mother and I was

thrilled at being a dad, but I knew in my heart that I had married for the wrong reasons. I wasn't in love with Mavis and, no matter how hard I tried, I soon saw that there was no way that I could make the relationship work.

Being in love with Sheree created other complications. Eddie started accusing me of not being able to concentrate on the job, and complained to our agent.

When I was called up to stand in front of Norman Murray and explain myself, I was flabbergasted. Apparently Eddie had told our office that Sheree was causing problems for Little and Large and something had to be done. When Norman met Sheree, though, he was so impressed with how lovely she was, he couldn't understand what Eddie was so upset about.

During the panto, Sheree was staying in a caravan with all her dancing friends. It was all pretty much above board, even when it came to helping her break into the caravan she was staying in because her friend had gone off with the key. As she climbed in through the window that night, I resisted the temptation to clamber in after her. A tiny kiss was all that was needed to send me on my way singing and dancing without the need for a stage or an audience.

After the panto, Sheree and I continued to see each other on a regular basis whenever we could. She was training for the ballet at the time and I would sit in the pub opposite the building where she took her dance classes until she had finished so that we could have supper together. We could chat for hours on end about all manner of things until we got chucked out by a tired pub landlord.

Two years after meeting Sheree, we got married. My divorce from Mavis was painful for everyone concerned, but I think we all felt that it was the right thing to do at the time.

It was a wonderful wedding, but, right up until the last moment, I was still having second thoughts. My decree nisi had just come through and I had a few wobbly days when I wondered if I was doing the right thing, but I would take one look at Sheree and all my worries and doubts disappeared.

As the parish church of West Houghton, near Bolton, was unwilling to marry us because I had been divorced, we went to the other end of the mining village and knocked on the door of the Methodist church there. It didn't seem fair that, because of my mistake, Sheree had to miss out on a church wedding, something that was important to her faith. She had attended the parish church since Sunday school days, but it still didn't seem to make any difference. We didn't want a register office wedding; we wanted to have God's proper blessing on our marriage.

The Methodist building, called the Bethel, was plonked in the middle of the high street, without any land surrounding it, and looked more like a telephone exchange than a church. Wrought iron gates gave way to a very bare interior with high set pews and no colour whatsoever. The coldness of the church building, however, was in total contrast to the warmth of the minister.

'I'd be delighted to marry you!' he said, with a chuckle that matched his girth, and I watched as Sheree's face turned into a naughty grin. She, her mother and the ladies from the Bethel were going to turn this drab-looking building into one of the most colourful and romantic places on Earth. It was the challenge of a lifetime, but Sheree relished it, even though she probably wondered if I would actually make it to the altar. Even the minister kept saying, with a twinkle in his eye, 'Is it on or is it off?' every time he spotted me.

When the moment arrived, it was a cold but sunny April day. It felt that God had sent all the spring crocuses and daffodils in little pots to come out and greet me as I arrived, almost as if they were saying, 'It's OK, Syd.'

Sheree arrived right on time, looking like a real angel in white. We stood at the front and, when I made my vows, I knew that I meant every word. If only I could have somehow underlined or highlighted each 'I do'! Now I know that I couldn't face life without her. It was as if God was saying that Sheree was the right one for me.

As I stepped out of the church and mingled with all the guests, my mother-in-law subtly crept up beside me, as they do, and said, 'Now, Syd. Marriages may be made in heaven, but there's a lot of hard work done here on Earth, too!' I smiled and nodded. It was a good lesson and one that I have always tried to put into practice on a regular basis since that day.

Sadly, Eddie didn't make it to the wedding because he was on holiday, but it turned out to be less of a showbiz event as a result and more of a family and friends day. Even my old mates Alf and Tony from an early band we called 'The Earwigs' turned up and it was great to see them enjoy themselves. My dear old mum had a whale of a time at the reception lunch.

'Cold meat, madam?' asked the waiter.

'Yes please,' said Mum.

'Vegetables, madam?'

'Yes please,' grinned Mum.

'Potatoes, madam?'

'Yes please,' smirked Mum.

Then she turned to me and whispered, 'I kept saying "yes" because he might ask me out next!'

'Mum! You're 72,' I said in shock and we all giggled.

We got to bed very late that night. At 5 a.m., we were up and in the car, on the way to our honeymoon. Sheree was saying how lovely it was to see everyone, but now we had some time just to ourselves and we could leave showbusiness behind for a while. Imagine the shock when we got to the airport and bumped into Tommy Hunt, a well-known entertainer of the day. I stood and chatted about the business with him until I knew I was trying even Sheree's great patience.

We eventually flew off to Tunisia and I made sure that when I came across any bands and comedians that week, I kept my face well hidden!

4

AUNTIE'S BLOOMERS

Four years and plenty of clubs later, *The Little & Large Show* began its life as a pilot television show for Thames Television. Eddie and I were pretty excited, but our agent Norman Murray dealt us a bit of a blow when he stormed into the public bar after we'd recorded the first show and bellowed:

'What do you think you two are doing? That was very amateurish!'

We were so embarrassed to be shouted at in public like this. I think he was trying to gee us on and make us sparkle even more, but, after flogging our guts out all week, to be told that we were useless just brought the usually strong Eddie to tears. Producer Royston Mayoh banned Norman from the studio from that day on.

The producer had passed the idea for the show to a team of executives looking for new talent for a Monday night entertainment slot. With a wonderfully funny sketch based on the song 'Smoke Gets in Your Eyes' where smoke billowed out to the point of making us feel like the studio was on fire, the pilot show was deemed to work well and a series was commissioned.

Opportunity Knocks had been running since 1956 – originally made by Associated Rediffusion, then by ABC and finally by Thames Television. It was ironic that as the long-running series that had made us famous was coming to an end, it was me and Eddie who were chosen to replace it. From 6.45 to the *Coronation Street* slot at 7.30 was now time that had to be filled and we were the ones to do it.

On the first day of rehearsals, Royston left a pile of scripts on the table for us to learn and it freaked us both out. 'This television series is going to be hard work,' I said to Eddie as we looked at each other in shock. No longer could we rely on the tried and trusted routines we had been performing in the clubs and theatres. Television was a hungry animal and once a sketch had been shown, that was it, it was never to be seen again. Of course we had a team of writers to help out, but it was the time and energy required to learn and time this constant flow of new material that really worried me. I was always concerned before a TV show because of this and the need to deliver a new sketch without a hitch. Eddie was always Mr Cool, but I would pace the floor of my dressing room, going over and over the words, actions and gags until they were coming out of my ears. Whereas Eddie could learn scripts in what seemed like one glance, it would take me ages. I even had scripts put down on cassette to play over and over on the long journeys between gigs. The atmosphere in the studio was often tense, because time was always short, so we were under a lot of pressure to make sure all the new laughter-making ideas worked well.

We must have done a pretty good job of it because at the end of our first series, while Thames Television were still deliberating about a second one, Michael Hurl jumped in with a contract from the BBC. This was not just another one-off, but a three-year deal. How could we refuse?

The series started off with a bang with good viewing figures and everyone seemed happy with the way in which our comedy worked for the cameras.

Norman Murray and his assistant, Ann, would still come to the studio, but just sit in the audience and watch. On one occasion during a camera rehearsal, they were spotted sitting reading the paper instead of watching the show, so Michael Hurl deliberately put the cameras on them so that everyone in the studio could see them looking so bored. We all had a laugh, but I don't think Norman and Ann realized what was happening. The moral to this story is that if you ever become part of a television studio audience, keep smiling!

This same year, we were invited to top the bill in our own summer show at Blackpool. On the bill with us was Norman Collier – to me still one of the funniest men around – Frank Carson – who still thinks he's the funniest man around – and a very young Jim Davidson – who was only on his first wife then. Eddie and I couldn't believe how fortunate we had become and on more than one occasion pinched ourselves to see if we would eventually wake up. We had never sought out fame, we just trotted along with what we knew worked on stage and succeeded in the nightly aim of making people laugh.

Getting the laughs was now becoming a serious business and we had to make sure that what we did was better and better each time we appeared. No longer could we rest on our laurels and say that if one live performance was bad, the next would be better. Our audiences' expectations had been raised and we realized that we had to be the best every time we appeared on that little box from now on.

I was proud and happy to be involved in the new series, but the fact that there were more scripts, more sketches and more material to work on sometimes put a downer on it for me. The more stressed out I got, the more mistakes I made. This frustrated Eddie, but that was me. Sometimes my mistakes and Eddie's quick-fire ad-libbing that got us out of the problem were funnier than the actual sketch we were doing. Sadly, being TV we always had to go back and re-record the original script, and so these extra bits never got shown.

It was arranged that, while we were performing our summer season dates, we would record the location material for the next series. Having got to bed after the stage show at about 2 a.m., we were often up again and in the mobile dressing room by 6 a.m., ready to costume up.

One morning, we were doing a very funny sketch that involved me and Eddie on the beach.

'I'm bored, Syd,' said Eddie, looking down at his feet and shuffling them. 'Can I bury ya?'

'Oh, OK,' said I with a sigh, looking up from my newspaper.

The next thing the viewer sees is a huge dumper truck full of sand with Eddie at the wheel. At this point I stopped the filming.

'Excuse me,' I questioned, 'I don't think I fancy this. You're not expecting me to actually get buried are you?'

'Oh. OK then,' sighed producer Bill Wilson. 'We'll have to use a dummy instead.'

I heaved a sigh of relief as the props department went to the costume lorry to have a look and eventually pulled out a very lanky-looking dressmaker's dummy.

'It doesn't look anything like me!'

'It will by the time we've finished,' they said.

Laying this poor mannequin on the ground, they attempted to dress it in my trunks and string vest, but its legs and arms were being thrown around all over the place and it was like trying to dress an octopus. A small wig was placed on the top, which kept falling off. I didn't feel well when they finally got a nail and hammered it straight into the skull. Then they asked me for my glasses.

'I think I've got a spare pair somewhere,' I readily offered – so glad that this fake Syd had agreed to stand in for me and worried that they may change their minds any minute.

Once the glasses were on, it did start to look a little like me and, from a distance, no one would have known it wasn't. The cameras then rolled and the instruction to Eddie to drive forwards was given as I stood at the side and watched. As he approached the dummy, I could see that the sand was soaking wet – the result of plenty of rain overnight. As the machine started to tip its heavy load on to the dummy, it was as if a hundred tons of sand was recreating a scene from ancient Pompeii. Suddenly there was a loud scraping metal noise and I watched with horror as the two arms used to double up as a forklift truck quickly swung forwards and chopped the head and legs clean off the dummy!

Apparently the owner of the dumper truck had forgotten to tie down the forklift legs and, as a result, everyone around me laughed, but my eyes were popping out of my head. I was in shock for some while, realizing that only a few minutes ago that was going to be me. After a strong cup of coffee and the sincere but dubious reassurances from Bill Wilson that he had always intended using a dummy, I was laughing, too. I could have been legless in a way that I'd never experienced before.

It crossed my mind that perhaps there was a secret plot to kill me when I was later asked to do a sketch involving a sinking ship. We all piled into this specially constructed garage on the South Coast near Torquay, where I was to sit at a table trying to get in touch with my dear departed Uncle Albert.

I was told that the idea of the gag was that, when I finally made contact, I would hear him say that he is aboard a ship and the garage would suddenly fill with water and a lifebelt with the words 'Titanic' on it would float past.

The first bit was manageable, but when the two hundred gallons of freezing cold water poured down from the over-head tanks directly above me, I thought I was going to drown. I was so cold that I couldn't stand up and, despite the fact that armies of crew members rushed up to me with towels, I was shaking so much they wouldn't stay on. For weeks afterwards my neck was stiff.

It was no better in the studio. One week we had the donkey that could count with its legs, the massive pink sow I had to

A large family holiday in Rhyl. I still 'like to be beside the seaside!'

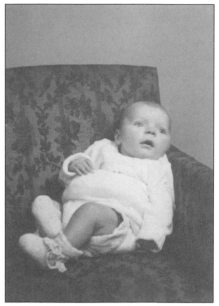

Even at a few months old, I'm singing!

Me, (on the left), aged seven, with Peter, David, Linda and the neighbours. Was I born with those NHS glasses?

One of our first publicity shots as 'Syd and Eddie'. We were so poor we couldn't afford second names!

Eddie the crooner and me showing early signs of wearing odd wigs. A dangerous thing to do in a Manchester club in 1961 and I was only 20!

Ten years later and the guitar and glasses remain. Those flared trousers are so old they're back in fashion now.

Summer Season in Scarborough 1975, with Dai Francis centre. Sheree is the first dancer in the line, far left.

A wonderful spring wedding. April 1975. Same trousers!

Status Quo guesting on our TV Series.

The TV Times launch of our first TV show on ITV in 1977.

Singing our hearts out with footballer Kevin Keegan.

Eddie seems enthralled by Elton John's kipper tie, but mine isn't any better!

Supersonic Syd.

Anyone seen my dressing room? Filming on location in 1980.

try to ride and the geese that jumped over miniature hurdles while laying unformed eggs. Then, another time, the doors of the rehearsal room in Acton swung open and in burst this creature, closely followed by its owner hanging on to its tail while being dragged across the floor looking as if he was waterskiing.

It was a kangaroo.

'What on earth are we going to do with that?' I asked Michael with an element of hesitation.

'Oh, it's a boxing kangaroo,' he said with a straight face. 'And you're going to box it!'

I had visions of me being flat on the ground within 30 seconds of the opening bell.

'Why me?' I protested. 'What's wrong with Eddie doing it?'

'Ah, he's going to be the referee,' came the carefully prepared reply.

Eddie smiled across at me and I looked back at this huge brown creature that, by now, had taken its keeper for a tour right around the room and was looking at itself in a large mirror. I am sure it spotted me standing behind, watching, because it turned and looked me straight in the face with an expression of loathing that I shall never forget.

Now I'm sorry to say that, in my book, kangaroos are not the nicest of God's creatures. Forget Skippy. This was more like a giant rat with fur more akin to a doormat than something nice and soft to cuddle up to. In fact, cuddling up to this creature couldn't have been further from my mind as we began to discuss what form this extraordinary exercise would take. All the while, I could see the kangaroo eyeing me up like an eager Frank Bruno, just waiting for the opportunity to get me in the ring.

'Ring! Yes, that's a good idea,' says Michael. 'We'll put Syd in a ring in the studio with the kangaroo and let them fight it out just like they would do at a real match.'

I couldn't sleep at all that night. Of all the things that I had been asked to do, this could be the funniest but also the most unpredictable. None of us knew what might happen once we got in the ring, least of all the trainer. Between the two of them I never quite worked out who was the boss.

The following day, I was in my dressing room at the studio at BBC Television Centre in Shepherd's Bush, when there was a knock at the door.

'We are ready for you now, Mr Little,' said the floor manager, with the hint of a chortle in his voice. I followed him silently out into the corridor, past the studio tea bar, and walked towards studio 2 as if I was a condemned man on Death Row. We went through the heavy swing doors and I was greeted in the studio with the biggest grin from Michael, who was obviously going to savour every single moment of what was about to happen.

'You look great,' he said viewing me up and down.

I was wearing a small pair of silk-like, black boxing shorts, a black and white vest, and my glasses. With the huge padded gloves on my thin little arms, they must have looked like matches with tea cosies on.

In the centre of the studio, they had erected a stage, surrounded by four bits of upright timber with three sets of rope attached. It didn't look very strong and I knew that if I were to fall against the ropes they wouldn't hold much weight. It wouldn't make much difference to the kangaroo of course; it could simply jump over the top!

The trainer took me aside and spoke to me for the very first time. 'Now listen, Syd. This is very important. You mustn't get too close to the kangaroo. What it will try to do is get its arms around your neck, pull you towards it and then bring up its powerful back legs and rip your stomach open.' This didn't sound much like the sort of pre-match talk that most trainers have with their protégés, but he went on:

'If you can manage to avoid letting it get a grip on you, everything will be fine and you will have nothing to worry about.'

Somehow I must have looked unconvinced because he added:

'Don't worry, Syd, he's used to all this. He's done it many times before.'

'Yes, but I haven't!' I nearly shouted back, but didn't as I wanted to avoid making a scene.

The sight for the audience was dramatic enough anyway. They sat there in silence as the warm-up man explained what was going to happen.

'How does he know?' I said to myself. 'I don't even know!'

I looked across at the ring to see my opponent climb or, rather, hop in. As I approached, it turned to look at me and I swear its mouth screwed up into a demented smirk as it chewed the cud like a bouncer chewing gum. On cue, I climbed into the ring and got my first shock.

'Where's Eddie?' I shouted.

'Oh, he's going to remain on the outside, doing the commentary,' said a disembodied voice from the studio gallery above.

'That's clever of him,' I thought. 'He's not stupid. His role change means he's out of danger and now I'm in here all alone with this weird beast.'

Well, after 20 minutes jogging backwards and forwards, trying to avoid the beast rather than encounter with it, nothing had really happened. A few giggles from the audience confirmed that it must have been quite an amusing sight, but nothing more.

'OK, take a rest everyone,' Michael called down from the gallery.

As soon as I dropped my hands to my side, whooosh, the kangaroo hit me.

Without hesitation and more by instinct than judgement,

I hit it back. The audience went bananas, shouting and cheering and clapping with excitement.

Michael appeared at the top of the gallery stairs and asked the floor manager what was happening.

'Well the kanga hit Syd and then Syd hit the kanga back,' he explained.

Michael's face instantly became a picture of misery and I thought he was going to burst into tears.

'What's the problem?' I asked.

'The cameras weren't running!' he replied.

And so one of the most incredible sketches on *The Little & Large Show* was only seen by a handful of people in a small studio in West London. I'm sure that, had it been filmed, it would have become one of the all-time favourites on *Auntie's Bloomers*.

As it happens, we did make it on to that show on a number of occasions anyway. The most frequently shown clip was of an extra playing a policeman. He only had one simple line to say, but the whole gag rested on it. Time after time, he messed up the few words he had until Eddie, in complete exasperation, said the line for him and the studio audience cheered with utter relief.

Another well-loved sketch was born when someone suggested that we could do something based on the popular children's characters Andy Pandy, Looby Loo and Teddy. So, in full costume, me as Andy and Eddie as Teddy, we leapt up and down on a giant bouncy castle that had been specially made by the television props and scenery department. The floor was painted like the surface of the Moon and we had supposedly taken a rocket-ride and ended up in space.

Michael was good at combining several ideas to give a sketch greater appeal and he dug out a song sent in by two bankers who fitted the scene for Andy and his friends perfectly. It's sung to the tune of 'Didn't We Have a Lovely Time the Day We Went to Bangor':

Wasn't it fun
To pick up a gun
And fill it full of water
Ol Looby Loo was tying her shoe,
She bended down
And whoops we caught her!

Her bloomers were pink
And didn't they shrink
I think her left leg's shorter
Didn't we all have a lovely time
Then we all fall down.

The material created in the studio didn't always work in the live arena, as we discovered to our peril when we tried to transfer this excellent sketch to the stage. It was to be one of our longest-running routines – we performed it for more than six years, on telly, summer season and pantomime. It was also the sketch that caused more backstage laughs than any of the others.

On another occasion, the motor pumping the air into the bouncy castle failed and the whole thing started to deflate. We did our best to keep going as the air rapidly started to disappear beneath us and bouncing became harder and harder. Eventually our feet were touching the floor and we pretended to bounce on our own before managing to finish the sketch. The audience must have thought it very strange.

Another night I arrived at the theatre with a severe case of the runs. I had been sitting on the loo all day and felt pretty awful, but I knew that the show must go on. The sketch I was most worried about was the Andy Pandy one, with all that bouncing.

'There's no way I'm going to cope with that,' I told the company manager. So they got our roadie, Dave, to put on the costume and take my place. 'No one will know,' they said, 'because the costume will hide his face and the song is recorded.'

There was no time for a rehearsal and when Dave got on stage and started to bounce, he really had no idea just how much energy he should put into it. As a result, he took enormous leaps and it looked as if he was on a trampoline. He overworked it so much and bounced so high that at one point Eddie thought he had disappeared up into all the equipment hanging from the ceiling. As I watched from the wings, tears of laughter began rolling down my face and I was giggling so uncontrollably that I had to rush to the loo once more.

When we were asked to do the sketch for Princess Margaret on *The Children's Royal Variety Performance* show, we were delighted. The details of the way in which the bouncy castle worked were sent to the production company at the Dominion Theatre and all looked well when we quickly inspected it before the performance. What we didn't know, however, was that the tray that the bouncy castle sat in had not been tied down and this oversight was to cause quite a stir.

As we began the sketch in front of a packed house and started to bounce in time to the music, I sensed that something was seriously wrong, but it was too late to stop now. Up and down we bounced, boing, boing, boing. As we did so, I suddenly realized that we were moving closer and closer to the edge of the stage. The whole castle was slowly making its way downstage and, any minute, we would be either in the pit with the orchestra or have floated out across the audience and perhaps out the back door! It was like being on a giant hovercraft and it seemed that there was nothing we could do about it.

Then, within a few inches of the orchestra pit, just when I began to see the whites of the eyes of an increasingly panicky conductor, a shout went up from the corner of the stage. On rushed six stagehands, who grabbed the giant inflatable and began dragging it back upstage just as the sketch drew to its close. The audience, thinking it was all planned, loved it of course, but I think the poor conductor was a nervous wreck for the rest of the night.

We loved to use a mixture of comedy and music as the basis for Little and Large. The most enduring way that we did this was when I would announce that I was fed up with him ruining our act with his silliness and I was going to redress the balance by singing a sensible song while accompanying myself on the guitar. The comedy element came as Eddie constantly tried to get in on the act, interrupting me at every possible opportunity. The climax came when Eddie realized that the only way to do this was to get a bigger, louder guitar than mine and so he marched on stage with an electric guitar that could be straight out of Status Quo. His attempts to play got louder and louder until he finally threw it on the floor and the amp blew up with great clouds of smoke. Perhaps this explains why, after 40 years standing in front of an exploding amp, my hearing is not as good as it should be!

This effect was achieved by a remote-controlled pyrotechnic device being carefully placed at the back of the amp and detonated by another roadie, Derek. A funny thing happened one night, after a season at Liverpool. A local stagehand called Norman had decided to play a last-night gag by pouring more powder into the device than normal to make a bigger bang.

As we worked in front of the cloth that would fly out ready for the guitar routine at the end, the stagehand was behind us, overfilling the pyrotechnic device in the amp. Unbeknown to him, in the wings, another stagehand saw that the plug required to power the system was not connected and instinctively pushed it into its socket. The resulting blast was enough to stop our act in mid flow and stun the audience into silence. How we carried on I don't know, but when we got off stage, there was a very blackened Norman, shaking like a leaf, being carried off to hospital. After treatment for burns, he was allowed home and, as far as I know, never tried to pull such a stunt again.

Many years later, when we were well known, we worked with Tommy Cooper again at the Palladium, this time on *The Royal Variety Show*. It was celebrating the Queen's Jubilee and was seen as America's salute to the Queen of England, so there were lots of American stars on the bill, such as Bob Hope and Shirley Maclaine, along with British names, including Brotherhood of Man and Tommy Cooper.

Other cousins from across the pond that year included the Muppets. They were brilliant and our roadie loved Gonzo – the mad one with a huge hooked nose who always seemed to get blown up. To Dave, Gonzo was his all-time hero. Like many others, Dave would sit engrossed, watching the Muppets at teatime on Sundays on ITV.

It was in 1976 that Jim Henson introduced *The Muppet Show*. The show was a phenomenal success, reaching an estimated 235 million viewers each week in more than 100 countries. It won three Emmys and many other awards during its five-year run. The bright colours and amazing antics won over audiences of young and old alike, so they were chosen to appear in this special *Royal Variety Show*.

I stood in the wings during rehearsals and watched Jim Henson standing behind a curtain with Gonzo hanging limply from his wrist. When Dave walked past, it was as if he has just seen his long-lost uncle.

'Gonzo!' he shrieked.

Suddenly, Gonzo sprang into life. It was almost as if Jim Henson had nothing to do with it. Here was a larger-than-life puppet on the end of someone's arm with a voice and a character all his own.

Dave was thrilled and had a conversation with Gonzo that lasted several minutes. I wondered if he was even going to ask him for an autograph when the stage manager called out for Mr Henson, and Gonzo and his manager were gone, leaving the biggest smile I have even seen on Dave's face. I wondered if the Queen would want to meet Gonzo after the show as well.

'It's a good job Sooty isn't your hero,' I called over to Dave. 'You wouldn't have got a word out of him!'

As the day wore on, everyone had finished their band call and the only person they were waiting for was Tommy Cooper. Most of the cast and musicians had gone home, and the only person left in the pit was Jack Parnell, the famous musical director of many a television variety show. Eddie and I were relaxing in the auditorium with a smattering of other acts, also waiting for the legendary Tommy to arrive.

It was just past midnight and the American directors were pretty frustrated by this time and ready to pack it in for the night, when a shuffling was heard on stage and the famous figure suddenly appeared, as if by magic.

'Mr Cooper, you should have been here at 12 o'clock!' shouted the directors from their production table in the stalls.

'But it *is* 12 o'clock,' retorted Tommy, pointing to his watch.

'No, we meant 12 o'clock, midday, Mr Cooper!'

'Oh dear,' said Tommy, raising his eyebrows.

All of us watching this drama unfold laughed our socks off, but I soon realized that we were the only ones doing so. The producers sat there with very stern and confused faces and I was reminded that American humour is different from our own. The two Americans just didn't get the fact that Tommy was pulling their legs, and this was just the start of it.

'OK, never mind, let's just rehearse. Close the tabs please and prepare for Mr Cooper's entrance!'

The stage manager closed the curtains, but, when they

opened them again, there was Tommy standing with his back to the audience.

'Mr Cooper. The audience is over here!' rang out an American tone.

'That's a gag!' explained Tommy as the two faces in the stalls stared back open mouthed in utter amazement.

'Jack?' said Tommy, leaning down towards the sole inhabitant of the pit. 'Will the music be a bit louder on the night?'

By this time, carpenters, dressers, stage door keepers and flymen were all coming out of their positions with tears running down their faces and the whole house was in uproar. All, that is, except the two Americans in the stalls, who still didn't seem to grasp what was going on.

At the end of the show, when the Queen and royal family came backstage to greet everyone. I seem to recall that she did smile at Jim Henson and Gonzo, but it was Tommy who gave her the biggest giggle. Just as she was walking away from Tommy, he said:

'Excuse me, Ma'am?'

'Yes?' she politely answered.

'Do you like football?'

'No' was the straightforward reply.

'Can I 'ave your FA cup tickets then?' he asked.

Only Tommy could get away with something as blatant as that. The Queen smiled once more and it was only the terrifying thought of meeting her next that kept us from collapsing on the red carpet with laughter.

The Queen slowly and professionally made her way along the line, asking the same question: 'And where are you working?' Then the Queen came up to me and Eddie and stood right in front of us. She was much smaller than we had imagined and looked us right in the eyes – from me to Eddie and then back again. As we were concerned not to break the protocol as Tommy had done, we firmly remembered that we had been told not to speak to the Queen unless she asked us a question.

The silence seemed to go on forever and we weren't quite sure what to do. I was just beginning to feel a little uncomfortable, then I realized that she was waiting for the Duke of Edinburgh and Prince Charles to catch up with her. A quick glance down the line confirmed that they were still in front of Tommy and both roaring with laughter. Eventually, they moved on towards the Queen, at which point she asked us the same question that she had asked all the others:

'And where are you working?'

After hearing Bob Hope say 'Las Vegas, Ma'am', Shirley Maclaine say 'Hollywood, Ma'am' and Jim Henson say 'New York, Ma'am', it was a huge anti-climax to declare 'Stoke-on-Trent, Ma'am', but it was true.

The Queen smiled sweetly and moved on.

When the Duke of Edinburgh arrived he was most concerned about the guitar slamming bit of our act:

'Was it really live?' he said. 'Was it still connected when it made that awful noise and sparks flew everywhere?'

It was nice that he was concerned about our safety and I was rather chuffed that he had actually watched us and not fallen asleep. Having been very impressed with the royal family, I also felt a little sad for them as I watched them walk away.

'I'd never want their job,' I said to Eddie as we prepared to climb the stairs back up to the dressing room we shared with others in the show. 'We've chosen to be in the public eye, but they haven't.'

Back in the studio, we soon learned the difference between timing on a live stage and in a studio. Although the show was always recorded in front of a live audience, Michael would always go back and edit the material to make it look its best and ensure that it ran to time.

He met us in the studio one day, looking a little agitated:

'You're not allowing enough time between gags,' he said.

We didn't understand because if a joke didn't get much of a laugh, we naturally went straight on to the next, as we would in a live setting. What Michael wanted us to do was to leave a gap where there should be laughs but nothing came – perhaps because the audience had missed it, were tired and there was no time to re-run something. We did as he requested and would sit at home watching the show saying, 'I don't remember *that* getting a laugh.' The penny dropped – Michael was putting laughter into all the gaps. This was particularly important when we were pre-recording material without an audience.

Our discovery that television is its own art form only made our admiration for the experts such as the stars of *Morecambe & Wise* and *The Two Ronnies* greater, but we must have done something right because our television show went on for 14 years!

By 1980, the television show was pulling in more than 16 million viewers each week and we were delighted that the audience was still laughing at our jokes after all these years. In fact, we carried on like this for the next nine years, until something happened that we could never have imagined.

5

SINGING IN THE MUD

Newfound fame and a little extra money is often something that people find difficult to cope with. For Eddie and me it wasn't such a problem and we did manage pretty well to keep our feet on the ground.

By now we were used to being recognized, but even this didn't go to our heads, perhaps helped by the sort of incident we had in a Chinese restaurant one night. Relaxing after the show over a chow mein, we kept seeing faces peer through a hole in the curtain that separated the main dining room from the kitchen. This was accompanied by a lot of chatter in Chinese and excitement. After a while, several very nervous waiters and waitresses came up to our table. One of the waiters had an autograph book in one hand and a camera in the other.

'Excuse me, but do you mine if we take a picture of you?' he politely, but hesitantly, enquired with a strong Chinese accent.

'Sure,' we said and posed together with our best smiles, hoping that no bits of onion were sticking out between our teeth.

'Thank you so much!' said the waiter afterwards. 'We love watchin' you on TV. It's I who noticed you here first,' he proudly announced. 'Look everyone, I said. It's the two Lonnies!' Moments like these keep you humble!

It was the special guest that we had on our television show each week that made it for me and meant that, at last, we could get to meet all those artists we had admired over the years. It was wonderful working with such musical legends as Lulu, The Searchers, Joe Brown and crooner Matt Monro.

We also had The Four Tops on one week and sexy popster Suzi Quatro. Her manager was Mickey Most – famous for being the grumpy one on the talent show *New Faces*. He made a career out of slagging people off well before *Pop Idol*'s Simon Cowell.

Mickey Most refused to allow Suzi to sing a comic song at the end with us, even though it was how we finished every show. Despite all the coaxing that the producers could muster, there was obviously no way she was going to sing. We were all disappointed and thought it would certainly look a bit silly if only The Four Tops did it, but decided we would go ahead anyway. However, as soon as Suzi's manager heard that the great Four Tops were joining in, he suddenly changed his mind. 'Someone's Knocking on the Door, Someone's Ringing the Bell' was the finale that week and to see Suzi in her leather gear, swinging her arms and hips next to us was a very satisfying finish for all concerned.

Gene Pitney was another favourite, as was Demis Roussos – otherwise known in the business as the singing marquee because he was so large. It was his first TV slot in the UK and, because we were in competition with the *Morecambe & Wise* show on the BBC to get the best guests, we celebrated when he chose us rather than Eric and Ernie.

It wasn't beyond me to put my foot in it with a big star either. We had Warren Mitchell on the show one week – famous for playing the wonderfully grumpy creation, Alf Garnett, in the hilarious sitcom *Till Death Us Do Part* on BBC. The connection was that one of our producers, Bill Wilson, had a son, William, who played the Garnett baby in the series.

In real life, Warren was as far removed from this unpleasant character as you could imagine, so it didn't sound too good when, after doing a sketch based in the East End, I shouted out 'Bye Alf' as he left the studio. He gave me a look that could kill and I had a face you could have toasted bread on. No wonder one of my nicknames is 'Loose-lips Little'.

Cher was only a guest because I played her. I wore a low-cut black dress with a body stocking that rode up very uncomfortably and boots. It was probably the most embarrassing and painful costume I ever had to wear. I drew the line when the make-up artist tried to insist that I had the tattoo put on my bottom to make it authentic.

What used to get me was that Eddie hated dressing up as a woman and, yet, when he did, he brought the house down – as he did when he came on as Tina Turner once. They would all say that I looked great, but somehow he always managed to play the romantic John Travolta parts and leave me to be Olivia Newton-John. One or two of the male dressers would get very excited whenever I had to dress in such a role and they would follow me all the way to the studio, as I wobbled along in high heels, making sure that nothing fell off along the way.

Some of the visual gags were made up or enhanced as we went along, but sometimes we needed instant props. These were supplied by the wonderful BBC props department, where they could get you anything from a wooden leg to a stuffed gnu at a moment's notice. For a spoof Spanish song, we suddenly decided we needed a real Spanish guitarist.

'I know one in a restaurant round the corner in Shepherd's Bush,' said a helpful member of the crew.

When Pedro arrived in the studio, he couldn't speak a word of English, so we all sang the song to him and, despite sounding like a load of croaking frogs, he managed to pick up the gist of the sketch. We wanted him to sing 'Guantanamera' in Spanish, so Eddie could do a comical translation of answers to the supposed questions.

'Yes, yes!' he kept saying, looking and sounding more like *Fawlty Towers*' waiter Manuel each time he did so.

We finished the rehearsal, the floor manager called a break and we all piled into one of the BBC refreshment areas located between each studio.

'He's great, he is.' Everyone was pretty impressed and most hadn't realized that we had just plucked him from around the corner. It was usual for ideas, scripts and gags to come from far and wide and from helpful members of the crew, though some were more helpful than others. As we sat around during the break, Eddie began developing an idea based on using the word 'eyes' in as many songs as possible and asked if anyone had any thoughts.

'I Only Have Eyes for You,' suggested a cameraman, sipping his tea.

'Smoke Gets in Your Eyes,' offered a lighting technician.

'Bright Eyes,' enthused the floor manager.

Then, from a small prop handler came 'Eye Shot the Sheriff?'

It was so funny and so stupid at the same time that the entire refreshment area collapsed in laughter and it was to take an increasingly irate director much time and patience to get us back on track to carry on filming.

An hour or so later, Eddie and I were called to the studio to commence filming in front of the live audience and, even then, someone spoiled the take by bursting into spontaneous laughter.

We managed to get through our opening piece, which went down really well, and, while the dancers were doing their number, we quickly changed into the costumes and made-up ready for the Spanish sketch. Any delay that keeps the audience waiting, even in a studio, carries the danger of losing the momentum and involves some effort to get it back again.

'Stand by!' said the floor manager. 'Three, two, one! Music!'

Silence.

'And music please!' he repeated with even more gusto, as if the guitar player was a little deaf.

Silence.

'What's going on? Where's Pedro?'

Suddenly, it was obvious that Pedro wasn't going to play ... because he wasn't there. He thought that the rehearsal was the actual recording and had left hours ago. Fortunately, they quickly found him – he was back in his restaurant, complete with guitar, crooning at the tables. The look on the diners' faces must have been a picture as our crew burst in with walkie-talkies, scripts in their hands and summarily picked him up and carried him off to the studio.

While all this was going on, it was the warm-up man who stepped into the breach and kept everyone laughing until Pedro arrived.

One of our warm-up men was a celebrity in the making. His name was Michael Barrymore. He had the same agent as us and so Norman Murray had suggested that we use him to get the studio audience from being cold and quiet to raucous and loud, ready for our sketches. The problem was that he did rather too good a job of it. By the time he had warmed the audience up, they were all laughed out and our sketches suddenly didn't seem so funny any more.

We'd booked Michael for our summer seasons and he was always a very good act, but he didn't have the opportunity to rule the roost there that he did in a studio setting. Norman, and Michael's wife Cheryl, were grooming him to become a big star and so any opportunity for him to work an audience, particularly in a studio, was taken.

'This isn't exactly helpful,' said Eddie one night, hearing the loud peals of laughter coming from the studio as we got ready for our first entrance. I must admit, it could have made the most confident comic waver a little, having to follow someone so funny, using polished material, with a new sketch they'd never done before in front of an audience and with no guarantee of a single laugh.

The first entrance was strong and we were greeted with the usual delighted whoops and plentiful applause. Several other sketches seemed to go down well and we began to think that we were being paranoid about Michael who, after all, we agreed, was only doing his job the best way he could. When it came to a point in the programme when there was a long break while we changed into complicated costumes and set up a large finale scene, it all changed.

Michael, by this time, had come to the end of his warm-up gags and, with his prepared material now exhausted, he decided that the only thing to do was to launch into his act. His act was totally hilarious and the element of throwing out members of the audience he didn't approve of was very new then. In seconds, the place was in an uproar.

When we came on and did our sketch, we died. As far as the audience was concerned, it was a complete anti-climax to what they had been watching and so, on our own show, it was the weakest finale we had ever done. In fact, it was deemed so bad that it was cut from the final edit and we had to do it again the following week. Needless to say, we found another warm-up man, but it wasn't long afterwards that Michael was given his own television series and perhaps it was born out of that day on *The Little & Large Show*.

One day, Michael Hurl attempted to lure us on to his new show idea called *Seaside Special*. He would produce this live event for the BBC, which would feature variety performers, dancers and several star acts. It was to be presented as a summer show and performed in a huge big top circus tent that was to be placed on a breathtakingly beautiful stretch of coastline, such as Bournemouth, Torquay, Yarmouth or Scarborough.

He asked whether or not we had decided to stay with Thames, but we didn't know, so he asked if he could approach our manager to work with the BBC. The next thing we knew, we got a three-year contract and *Seaside Special* was a series of one-offs for us. It was a great success and ran for many years, but we found it to be a complete illusion. It wasn't live, set by the coast or filmed in the summer. In fact, the first time we did the show, it was freezing cold and it was raining so much that we shivered before we went on stage.

Michael kindly brought the tent up to Manchester, where we were already doing a season, and plonked it in the middle of a car park in Belle Vue. It was mid November, but we all had to pretend it was a summer's day in July, despite the fact that the rain was making the noise of an aircraft landing on the tent roof. It had rained from five o'clock the previous morning right up until the moment we began recording and there were very real doubts that the event would still go ahead. Indeed, as the rain continued to pour down all day, we rehearsed surrounded by mud and the crew dug a moat around the tent to try to draw the enormous amounts of water away. By the evening, we were all hanging around, wondering if the rain would stop, and, when I glanced at one of the television monitors, I could see that the cameramen were focusing their cameras on hundreds of polystyrene cups floating along mini rivers under the seats in the auditorium.

While the lighting riggers climbed up tall ladders to tip up the huge television stage lights and to relieve them of the water that had collected inside them, the stage crew started to put tons of sawdust down on the floor. It was supposed to soak up the water, but it just turned into a mush, and we felt like we were wading through semolina.

'All we need is a nice knob of jam and we'll be well away,' I said to Eddie, but he didn't smile.

When the audience arrived, they wore surprised faces and sloshed around in their seats. I was amazed that so many had turned up in such bad weather, but I suppose it was a free show! Looking forlorn, they were soon told to cheer up and look as though it was a lovely hot summer's day outside. Then, as if on cue, the rain stopped and the orchestra started.

Unfortunately, although the rain had stopped, the mud remained. The caravans that were used as dressing rooms were out in the car park and, by the time the girls scrambled out there between numbers, changed, and made their way back through the swamp, they were covered in mud again. I watched as one poor girl tried to wipe away streaks of brown grime from her fishnets with a tatty tissue before bouncing back on to the stage, all smiles.

The wet and mud weren't the only problems. The huge industrial heaters they had installed at the sides to blow out hot air and eradicate the damp didn't do any of our hairstyles any favours. We all went on stage looking rather windswept that night and at least one act I know nearly lost his toupee.

Marti Caine was also on the bill and a very clever comedienne. We had originally seen her in a working men's club in Sheffield. She came on looking like she was a glamorous dancer, but then surprised everyone with her risqué jokes and powerful voice. The band Smokie, of 'Living Next Door to Alice' fame, were also on the show, as was Leo Sayer and it was nice to work with someone a bit smaller than us!

Eddie and I did a great Laurel and Hardy routine. We had a trick model T Ford that we danced and sung around as a centrepiece. Bits of the car would blow up as we sang, but the final bit of magic was when the lights of the car exploded and one of them actually landed right on top of Eddie's head. The odds of that happening must have been millions to one and encouraged the audience to yell and clap even more than usual – the place was in uproar.

This piece is still regularly shown today, but, apart from the amazing exploding car, watch out for some very muddy stage trousers and some unusual-looking hairstyles!

By this time, the creative Michael Hurl had justifiably been

nicknamed 'The Boy Scout' and we would give him an appropriate salute any time we passed in the corridor! He was such
a fast-moving, workaholic producer, doing *Seaside Special*
or *The Little & Large Show* one minute and *The Two Ronnies* or *Top of the Pops* the next, that the joke eventually
became, 'When Michael Hurl dies and goes to heaven, he'll
see his life flash before him, badly edited!'

I'm certainly glad that Norman Murray, our agent, wasn't
there that day. He still seemed to us to be a really hard man.
He hadn't softened at all in the years since we started working
with him in 1977. On one occasion at the Alexander Theatre
in Birmingham, we were in the middle of rehearsing a new
panto and sitting in our dressing rooms listening to the show
being relayed on the tannoy. They were obviously having
some trouble hearing the 18-year-old girl playing Cinderella
because we suddenly heard Norman scream, 'Get the cow
near the mic!' The panto's director then burst on the scene
and we heard what seemed to be him trying to throw Norman
out of the building. It was just like listening to a radio farce.

It was in this same panto season that another act showed
jealousy of our success. When we had first arrived at the
venue, we bundled into our respective dressing rooms, ignorant of the fact that another comedian on the bill had changed
all the dressing room numbers around to make sure that
he got number 1. Consequently, number 1 dressing room
became number 5 and number 2 became number 7 and it
wasn't until the end of the season that Eddie and I discovered
why our rooms were more cramped than normal!

Another sticky moment was when we popped in to see our
mate Stu Francis at the Britannia Theatre, Great Yarmouth.
We couldn't stay to see the show in the evening because we
were working, so we thought we would just pop in to see
him rehearse. We had just settled ourselves down in the auditorium when we heard a huge voice boom out towards us.
It was Dickie Hurran, a brilliant variety director, but not

someone known for his manners. He was always immaculately turned out, complete with a fresh red carnation in his buttonhole, but his way of dealing with people wasn't so friendly.

'Who's there?'

'Little and Large.'

'What do you want?'

'Just to watch our mate, Stu, Mr Hurran.'

'He's working till five o'clock. Come back then.'

He refused to continue until we left, but Eddie remembered this incident for years afterwards. When we were booked to do a major summer show and it was suggested that a Mr Dickie Hurran would direct us, we refused. I think it was the first time Dickie was ever turned down, but revenge was sweet.

We didn't tell Norman any of this or else he would have gone berserk. As an agent and manager, you have to be tough with all the sharks that inhabit the business side of the theatre, but you need to be a lot gentler with the performers! Such experiences were not good for us and, eventually, by the mid 1980s, we agreed to part company with our agent.

Eddie knew that his best mate, Jimmy Tarbuck, had a good agent called Peter Pritchard and so he was an obvious first choice to call. Peter, a London agent, took us out to lunch one day and said that he would love to manage us. He soon inherited us and got to work renegotiating our television and theatre work. Peter was to be a good agent for us and expertly kept our career going, right up to the present day.

Peter got us bookings as guest appearances on programmes such as the *David Nixon Magic Show*. David was a tall, bald, well-spoken gentleman and very polite. He invited us to his house one day, along with some other friends, and showed us all round. Eddie and I were so surprised because he kept showing us how much of the alterations and refitting he had done himself. He must have had more than enough money to get people in to do it for him, but he just loved making things.

'I love doing DIY,' he exclaimed, showing us a sparkling new kitchen, but to me David just didn't strike me as that way inclined. When he showed us a swimming pool he had put in himself, we began to wonder if he was just kidding us.

'I bet he hasn't done any of this,' I whispered to Eddie. 'He's waved his magic wand and it has all just appeared!' Eddie gave me one of his looks.

When David left the room to make us all some coffee, we sat chatting in what was a huge room. Someone pointed out towards the enormous garden.

'Do you like the back yard?' he said. 'It's called Sussex!'

Celebrity Squares was always great. An old ITV game show that ran from 1975 to 1979, it was revived in 1993 for two years and was hosted by Bob Monkhouse on both occasions. It was essentially a hi-tech version of noughts and crosses. Viewers used to think that camera trickery was involved in making the grid of nine little boxes, each lit up and containing a celebrity, but it was for real. Being a double act meant that we both had to climb up the rickety steel ladder at the back and squeeze ourselves into the box. It was a bit tight and I used to worry about falling out of the front or the back.

Once in position, each celebrity was asked a question and the contestants had to say if their response was correct or not. If they got it right, they won the square and the aim was to win a full line. Lots of fun ensued, with the questions encouraging plenty of comic ad-libs. Dudley Moore was on the same programme as us and completely stole the limelight with his quick wit.

We loved being on *Noel's House Party*, too, where a 'ding dong' at the front door was followed by Noel inviting us into his mansion in the fictional village of Crinkly Bottom and we were greeted with a huge roar of welcome from the studio audience. My favourite moment was when I appeared as a bus conductor and Eddie was the driver. We had supposedly brought a busload of strange people to Crinkly Bottom, which gave Eddie a good excuse to do some of his wildly funny impressions.

Noel Edmonds, the show's creator, producer and presenter, always impressed me. The series was ahead of its time in terms of fast-moving light entertainment shows and included wonderfully creative elements, such as NTV, where a hidden camera was set up in an unsuspecting viewer's home, 'Wait Till I Get You Home', where kids embarrassed parents by telling stories about them, and 'Grab a Grand', where a personality grabbed as many bank notes as possible in a windswept glass booth for a lucky viewer – all well before reality TV was ever heard of.

It also spawned the gunge tank, where viewers voted for celebrities to be covered in brightly coloured goo, and, of course, the excellent Mr Blobby. I think you either loved him or hated him, but he was certainly a larger-than-life character. I got on quite well with him actually.

Not only was the show full of variety, while managing to remain topical, but Noel was a snazzy dresser. It didn't seem to matter whether he was in front of the cameras or not, he was always immaculately dressed. Off stage I'm a bit more relaxed about what I wear, but when we arrived for the rehearsals for another appearance on the programme, Noel took one look at me and said:

'Syd, that's the same shirt and jacket you were wearing last time I saw you!'

He seemed genuinely concerned, but I wasn't bothered one iota, just stunned that Noel had even noticed what I wore.

Noel's House Party also featured the famous 'Gotcha'. When it was our turn, my job was to lure Eddie into a local restaurant where another planted guest had to try to wind Eddie up to bursting point. Apparently Noel's team had picked up a bit in the newspapers about an alleged story involving Eddie with a car, a broken windscreen and a set of golf clubs.

'My girlfriend thinks you're great,' said the man coming over to our table and leaning over him menacingly. Eddie just smiled.

'Will you do some impressions for me?' came next.

Eddie looked at me, then back at the man and obliged as best he could. The man laughed then went over to a counter and got a telephone.

'Can you do your impressions for my girlfriend? She's on the phone,' he said, handing the receiver over to Eddie.

Eddie frowned, but didn't lose his cool. I was so surprised and wondered if he had guessed what was going on.

'Can you sign these for me?' was the next question, as the stranger handed Eddie a handful of beer mats.

Eddie just went along with it all, but I could see from his face and agitated body language that he wouldn't take much more and I expected him to walk out at any minute.

The producers had told me just to stay put with Eddie and behave as if nothing was awry and so I did, desperately trying to think of ways in which to keep the conversation going. I had almost run out of ideas when a strange man in a gorilla outfit arrived, wheeling in a birthday cake. That was when Eddie blew.

'You ******!!'

His words had to be bleeped out as it was family viewing, but his arms swung about wildly. Noel managed to duck out of the way of any blows, but did not escape Eddie's fingers, which ripped the gorilla mask off.

'I'll get you back, Noel! You just wait!' Eddie's revenge had already started to form in his mind. Sadly, *Noel's House Party* finished a few months later and so the threat is still outstanding. Watch out Noel!

Eddie's 'Gotcha' became one of the top three most popular

of the entire series, which ran until March 1999 – almost nine years.

Despite the fact that Noel obviously had reservations about my dress sense, we were invited back for the last programme of the series, where it seemed that the whole of the celebrity world had turned out to celebrate the event. This even included Oliver Reed. This legendary actor, infamous for being the worse for wear when alcohol was around, spent the whole day in the studio walking around with a brandy bottle in his hand. It was so odd to see this wonderful actor behaving like this and I told myself that it must all be an act. Come the evening shoot, he had disappeared.

The party in the green room afterwards was a wonderful chance for everyone in the series to let their hair down, though it was quite odd seeing several special guests from ITV's *The Bill* disco dancing!

The regular combination of television, pantomime and summer season shows meant that, by now, we were in the big earnings' league. Not that we saw much of it! Our accountant gave us what amounted to pocket money each week and kept the rest back. Unfortunately, we found out later that this lump sum was never invested properly and so, when a huge extra tax bill for £360,000, going back over 10 years, suddenly came in because the accounts had been mishandled, it wiped out all our savings and pensions in one fell swoop.

Leonard Courts, of Maurice Apple Accountants, came in, sorted it all out and put us back on an even keel. Although we had nothing left, we decided not to cry over spilt milk and it was like starting again. The only problem was that, by this time – the late 1980s – the work was starting to slow down.

Things were also changing at the BBC. Although we aimed to be a quick-fire laughter and entertainment show, it seemed that we were starting to become controversial, albeit unintentionally. The worst effects of political correctness were just starting to be felt at this time and went on to sound the death knell for a lot of comedy. This is because comedy is essentially about laughing at ourselves. We tell gags about age, about jobs, about grandmas and grandpas, parents and children, about relationships, about everything, really. If parts of life become no-go areas, it all starts to fall apart. Suddenly, we had to put a big question mark over everything that we did and when you start to question comedy, it loses its funniness. I do agree that comedy should never be used to hurt or degrade people, but it must involve seeing how silly we human beings really are.

The silliness of it all was underlined when we had a lovely Indian actor called Albert Moses take part in a sketch of ours that involved him being the manager of a sitar band. Eddie and I played the instruments, but were not pretending to be Indian, which was part of the joke. Albert played the archetypal Indian manager of the band beautifully and it got great laughs in the studio.

The next week, the mailbag, which usually attracted comments about how many people had enjoyed the show, contained several letters condemning us for making fun of Indian people. The writers of the letters had obviously not realized that Albert really was Indian! It saddened me that people had read in to the sketch ideas that weren't actually there or ones that weren't intended to be there.

On one programme, we were berated for having several weeks with different ethnic minorities on and then one week with just white people on. Again, we didn't do this on purpose; it's just the way it happened. Whatever we did now, it seemed more and more important that the criticisms of a small, but loud, minority of people in the BBC were heard rather than us focusing on the entertainment value for the millions. After all, Eddie and I are red-nosed comics, not politicians!

I have good friends right across the spectrum of race and never have I heard any of them complain to me about any of our sketches or gags, so what they were saying to us at the BBC made no sense to me. Gradually things got worse and worse as a result of a whole range of incidents. On one occasion, Eddie and I were appearing on a Saturday morning children's programme with Keith Chegwin in which they showed a clip to plug the show being transmitted that night. The gag was that Eddie was supposed to be on a diet and I came into the kitchen and caught him red-handed, cooking something in the microwave.

'You're supposed to be on a diet,' I said. 'So whatever you've got in there I'm going to eat myself!'

Eddie then pulled open the door to reveal a hot-water bottle. The whole studio on that early Saturday morning laughed, then we finished our interview and prepared to leave. Just as we got to the door, there was a whole lot of commotion going on and the floor manager rushed up to us all breathless. He said:

'We need you to go back and tell the children watching that they mustn't put hot-water bottles into microwaves!'

We sort of understood what he wanted us to do and why, but it would have looked really foolish for us to have made a Batman and Robin-type announcement about the dangers of hot-water bottles. We couldn't believe how silly this would be and at first Eddie refused to do what they asked, saying:

'If you take that to its logical conclusion, it means that if you can't do anything in a sketch for fear of someone copying, you can't do anything at all!'

Despite our protests, the producers demanded that we went on at the end and do a 'Don't try this at home . . .' announcement – 'Kids. Do not put a hot-water bottle in a microwave because it's dangerous . . .'

We talked of a nightmare scenario, that we'd have to do

after every sketch. 'Don't play on the beach, it's a dangerous place!' I thought should follow our dumper truck sketch. Maybe we'd even have to say 'Be careful of banana skins as you walk along the pavement'!

Strangely enough, we weren't too far wrong. Later, we did a sketch involving an ice-cream van, with Eddie inside and a small child ran up to ask for a cornet, but he hadn't got enough money. The kindly man waiting in the queue, played by me, offered to buy it for him instead, and the child went off, licking his lips and with a big beaming smile.

Then another child came along, and another, and another, and the same kind gentleman paid for every one. At the end of the sketch it turned out that the ice-cream man in the van was getting all his own kids to come out and get me to buy the ice-creams. It was a very funny sketch, but we were instantly in trouble for encouraging children to accept ice-creams from strangers.

Even though we pointed out that the parent was involved in the plot, the BBC aired the sketch on its *Points of View* programme, then presented by Anne Robinson. Eddie and I couldn't understand why the BBC was knocking its own popular shows, even ones with eight million viewers! That's the sort of support we needed like a hole in the head.

Things were starting to get beyond what we considered sensible and appropriate. Television comedy was on the verge of great change. These days, I think comedy has gone too far. It seems that all you have to do is shout a four-letter word and people will laugh. Some live shows use nudity and foul language, which to me is far more offensive than anything Little and Large even dreamt about!

These days, the technique of using sketches and variety has all but disappeared and the art of cajoling, rather than shocking, an audience into submission is nearly extinct. Yet, I believe that's what the audience still wants. It explains the huge popularity of the reruns of classic comedy sitcoms, Morecambe and Wise and Tommy Cooper. These great family comedians have never been replaced.

The Little & Large Show finally threatened to come to an abrupt end in 1989 when we were invited out for a celebration meal after the last live recording. James Moir, the head of light entertainment, along with all those who had been involved in the 12-year long series, joined us, including our agent, Peter Pritchard.

After a lovely meal at The Savoy, we were each handed a wine glass inscribed with an 'S' or an 'E'. We didn't realize until much later that the sincere thanks given to us over the table was the BBC's way of saying goodbye.

A nice addendum to the television story was when Peter Pritchard telephoned a few months later.

'You won't believe this, Syd, but the BBC want to do another series.'

Apparently they couldn't find another act to fill the spot we had vacated and we ended up doing another two years, taking us to 1991. They still hadn't found a replacement, but they obviously thought it was time for us to go and, although we were sad, we had enjoyed a very lengthy run, so we couldn't really complain, could we?

Were audience numbers down? No.

'Those shows you've done over 14 years, Syd,' said James Moir as we were leaving for the last time. 'Those repeats will be your pension fund, you know.' I looked at him quizzically and his words never came true because *The Little & Large Show* has sadly not seen the light of day since. It's true to say that, to date, no other light entertainment show, apart from *Morecambe & Wise*, has been repeated in its entirety either. It's a shame because the era that produced the greats – from Harry Worth to Cannon and Ball – and a host of others could still be enjoyed today. As the whole shape of television entertainment began to change, *The Little &*

Large Show became one of the last variety shows of its type. We walked away from the security of what had been a long-lasting, well-paid job and wondered what lay ahead.

6

TRAGEDY AND TRIUMPH

'Get mad, Cliff!' Eddie and I urged as we sat in the stalls and watched a disaster unfold.

It was an interesting start to our first season with Cliff Richard at the London Palladium in 1974 – not least because at rehearsals everything had been going wrong. The lights were flashing in the wrong places, the sound was terrible and poor Cliff's mic kept breaking down. Cliff, however, remained calm throughout.

It was the first time I began to wonder what his secret was. I knew that he had a strong personal faith, but I didn't realize belief in an invisible God could have such an impact on the personal and professional side of anyone's life. I chatted briefly with him about this in the wings during the next few weeks in which we worked together, but it wasn't so much what he said that impressed me, but how he actually lived his life. I promised myself that I would try to live like that if I ever got the chance.

A few years later, I saw that same sense of inner peace in the midst of the storm in dear Roy Castle. Roy was an amazingly, incredibly talented man who was the best all-round entertainer I had ever seen. We had him on our show as a guest several times and it was always a joy working with him because of his professionalism and ability to be so generous a performer to those he was working with. Eddie and I were devastated when we heard the news of his lung cancer, probably contracted as a result of playing the trumpet and so deeply inhaling the smoky atmosphere of countless late-night clubs and cabaret venues.

As I watched Roy join the Train of Hope to raise money for his cancer fund to provide more research into the disease, I couldn't believe my eyes. There was a very sick man, willing to put himself through the personal and public agony of such a long journey, just to benefit others. Everywhere he went he was on the news and in the papers. Not once did I see him frown. Despite feeling, and probably knowing, that he was so near death, his face sported a smile the whole time.

'Whatever he's got that makes him cope, I want some of that,' I promised myself again. Little did I know that the same God who was helping Roy through was preparing me for my own personal pain.

It was in 1994 that we were in panto at the lovely Wimbledon Theatre. One afternoon, I got a knock at the door and in walked a man with a big smile who said:

'Hello, Syd. I'm Chris, from Christians in Entertainment. I've heard that you are a bit of a churchgoer and so I've come to offer our support and prayers.'

It was true. Chris had picked up on a snippet in the newspapers that had reported our family move to Torquay and the fact that I now attended St Matthias' Church in nearby Babbacombe. In fact, my desire to know more about the God of Roy Castle and Cliff had led me back to my church roots and, under the guidance of the vicar, Peter Larkin, I had even been confirmed, at the age of 50!

We were involved in the church as much as we could be, given the fact that I was away such a lot. We even suggested to the Parish Council that we hold a karaoke night to raise money for church funds.

'Sorry, Syd, but what's a karaoke?'

Amazingly, they hadn't heard of this fun practice of singing along to a backing track, but I promised that I would help them out and show them what to do. We had a hilarious time, with the church secretaries and treasurers letting their hair down for what seemed to be the first time in years! I've heard it even got Peter Larkin going and that he's wanted to sing from the pulpit ever since. Perhaps he can become the first vicar to sing a sermon?

'Nice to see you, Syd!' said Chris, who seemed to leave just seconds after he had arrived.

It was rather a nice introduction, really. Eddie and I would only invite people up to our dressing room we were sure of. Once inside, it is sometimes difficult to get rid of unwelcome visitors, so the dressing room has to be a very private space. If Chris had outstayed his welcome or started to preach at me, I would probably have asked Derek, our roadie, to help him on his way, but I suspect Chris knew that.

A few weeks later, Chris called back. He had been seeing someone else in the cast and popped in to see me as well. This time he stayed a short while longer and then said:

'Shall we have a quick pray before I go?'

'OK,' I said, not sure what I had let myself in for, but his prayer was short and to the point:

'Dear God. Please continue to be with Syd on stage and off. May he know that you care for him and will look after him in all that happens to him this week. Amen.'

Although a short prayer, it was to be perhaps the most poignant one of my life for, a few days later, there was a different knock at my door.

'Hi, Dad.'

It was Paul, my son, now 26 years old.

Paul had been a difficult child from the beginning. Some blamed my lifestyle and divorce for his behaviour, but I think it was an even deeper problem than that. Paul was always getting into trouble with the police and Mavis would ring me each time to tell me that he had either been expelled from school for the third time or had been caught stealing sweets from the local shop.

When he was nine years old, he was involved in an accident – a delivery van knocked him down in the road. He was rushed to hospital and recovered, but I feel that he was never the same after that. Sometimes he would scream and swear and other times he was as good as gold. His behaviour was very inconsistent.

'They're killing me, Dad!' was a call I got from Paul while we were recording our television show one day.

The operation on his leg to try to correct it for a lack of growth must have been a very unpleasant experience for him. They had to break the bone, then insert a metal frame that would keep the bones apart to encourage new bone to grow and eventually close the gap. Every way Paul turned in his life, there seemed to be a problem and I seemed so unable to help. I would have liked to have got in the car and driven up north to see him then and there, but I couldn't.

Over the years, things continued to go from bad to worse and eventually, unbeknown to me, he began to dabble in alcohol and drugs. He was just 12 years old when he started to experiment with marijuana. From there he apparently met someone in a pub who offered to help him feel better and introduced him to heroin. I was told that usually drug users go to cocaine first, but Paul made a huge leap up the drug ladder and was soon firmly hooked at the most dangerous level.

During this time, he had an occult sign tattooed on his forehead.

'Why did you have that done, Paul?' I asked him one day.

'Don't know, Dad,' he said. 'Must have been when I was stoned.'

When he got fed up with the circular emblem, he couldn't have it erased, so he tried to grow his hair long enough to cover it.

I heard from Mavis that he jumped in front of a car while playing some sort of dare game when under the influence of drugs, believing that he would be invincible. He wasn't of course. It seemed that he would do anything to gain as much attention as possible.

In his late teens, Paul was diagnosed as schizophrenic and was then placed in one mental institution after another. Periods of being out in the real world were followed by spells in these places, usually after some sort of petty crime spree. Mavis tried to shield me from the increasingly inquisitive press. So I don't think she told me everything that Paul got up to. She knew that Paul would also suffer as a result of any stories written about him in the media.

Alongside the treatment for his mental illness, attempts were made to dry him out and put him through cold turkey to get him off drugs. The techniques used in those days were not as advanced as they are today and must have been pretty distressing.

Paul had been in an institution in Leicester before he was moved to a mental home in Prestwich, Manchester, where I went to see him one day in 1993. As I walked into the huge concrete block of a building, full of strange smells and noises and an atmosphere of terror hanging in the air, it was almost too much and I was tempted to turn around and leave. The gargoyles on the walls outside and the clanging of the door behind me as I moved inwards didn't help. It felt more like a prison than a hospital. I searched the wards for Paul without finding him and so asked a nurse for some help.

'That's Paul over there,' she smiled, pointing in the direction of a lad sitting at a small wooden table painting a ceramic pot. He looked so different that I hadn't even recognized my own son.

'Hello, Paul,' I said.

He barely looked at me and I wondered if he knew who I was.

'Paul, you shouldn't be in here. You're young. You could be out making a family and living life to the full.'

'Got any money for me ciggies, Dad?' was his only reply.

He used to smoke Royals, the cheapest available. I looked at his new Rastafarian hairstyle, and sensed that my words were simply evaporating into thin air rather than reaching him. It felt like I was talking to a brick wall.

Every time I went to see him in the next few weeks it was the same. It was as if Paul was drifting further and further away. He wasn't my son any more. He was becoming someone else and the tears I cried in the car after each visit were endless. The whole experience of visiting him was becoming so distressing, that I think I made a psychological decision not to see him any more. Excuses as to why I couldn't go back flowed easily from this point, while feelings of guilt and helplessness left me lonely and empty and craving to get back to the comparative security and reassurance of a stage. Consequently, when he turned up that day at Wimbledon Theatre, I hadn't seen or heard from him in many months. Paul was able to convince anyone of anything, so this must have been why the board at the institution had decided that he was well enough to leave, I thought.

'They let me out a while ago, but I've stolen a pair of jeans, Dad,' he explained. 'The police say that I've got to go back inside, but I really want to have a holiday before that. Have you got some money to help me, Dad?'

How could I resist such a request from my son?

'Sure, come back tomorrow and I'll have it ready for you, Paul.'

The following day, at exactly the same time, the telephone in my dressing room rang once more.

'Your son Paul is at the stage door, Syd. He's asking for you.'

I looked at the clock on my whitewashed dressing room wall. It was midday.

'That's fine, just send him up,' I requested.

'He's asking that you come down and see him', was the reply.

Odd, I thought, as I descended the concrete stairs to the stage door.

'He's outside,' gestured the stage door man.

'Hi, Paul.'

'Hi, Dad.'

We stood looking at each other for an uneasy moment in the side street as the world bustled past.

'Have you got the money, Dad?'

'Sure,' I handed him a cheque. 'But you do promise it's for a holiday?'

'Of course. I love you, Dad.'

With that he was gone. I climbed back up the stairs to my dressing room with bewilderment in my mind and heaviness in my heart.

The next day, I parked my car in the theatre car park and wandered along to the sandwich shop to buy some lunch. As I passed the newsagents next door, something involuntarily made me glance sideways. There on the metal newspaper stand was a headline that wrenched my stomach.

'Syd Little Pay-off – "Get out of my life", he says to his son', or something like that. To be honest I was so dazed by the whole thing, I can't remember the words exactly to this day, but the hurt I felt went down like a knife into my soul. It was just so untrue.

It was obvious that Paul, my own son, had set me up. He not only got the money that I gave him, but a large sum from the newspaper for the bogus story as well. As I went through the details of his visit in my mind, other things began to fall into place. While giving Paul the cheque, a photographer must have been hidden in a car across the street, clicking away. The result was a rather distorted front-page picture of me handing Paul the money. That was why Paul had asked me out into the street, rather than see me in the privacy of the theatre.

'Don't retaliate or it will just fan the flames,' advised Eddie. 'It'll make the story run for weeks.'

I agreed and decided to stay silent on the whole issue. This wasn't easy either. Some people must have assumed that because I didn't come out fighting for my corner, it must be true. The problem was I didn't know of an honest platform available for me to put my own story across.

The newspaper tried to continue the story and even made comments in another article based on the question: why doesn't Syd give Paul a chance? Again, the truth about the whole issue was never aired, but it is now!

I tried to put a stop to the cheque, but it had already been cashed and, with the money that Paul had now banked, he left the country.

A year later I was at home when Sheree called up the stairs to tell me that Mavis had called and that it sounded urgent. It was 1995.

'I'm sorry, Syd,' said Mavis when I finally managed to get through. 'But Paul has been found dead in a hotel room in Bangkok.'

I couldn't believe what she was saying and I suppose it still wasn't a reality for me until his body was brought back from Thailand and we buried him in Sale, Manchester, where he had spent most of his childhood. His grave has become something of a shrine, with his picture there, and I hope it can be some sort of a reminder to others how terrible drugs can be.

I suppose it wasn't a surprise. Several people had been saying that there was only one way that Paul would go if he carried on the way he was. The drugs had such a hold on him that there was very little chance of escape.

Throughout this time, I had to continue going out on stage and making people laugh. An audience expects a comic to never be ill and certainly didn't want to know about my personal life. The people come to see Little and Large so that they can get away from their own pain and life's difficulties. I had a duty to perform, but I couldn't have done it alone.

Alongside the support of close friends and family, there was a new inner strength beginning to emerge. It reminded me of Cliff and Roy and the inner calm that I so clearly saw make such a difference to their lives.

As I prayed to God, I asked that he support me at this time of tragedy and show me the way forward. The answer came immediately when a total stranger stopped me in the street a few days later.

'Syd. I'm so sorry to hear about Paul,' said the lady with a smile. 'But we are praying for you.'

I had letters saying similar things from all over the place and Chris called to say that whole churches around the country were praying, too. I did indeed feel that God's love surrounded me, that he was carrying me and was going to get me through.

I think that one of the people who suffered most from Paul's short but difficult life was Donna, my daughter. She was bullied mercilessly by him and, because so much attention was demanded by Paul, Donna was sidelined a lot of the time.

Three months after Paul's death I got a surprise telephone call from my agent.

'Have you spoken to Donna recently?' he asked.

'Not for a while, no,' I said, wondering why a man in his position should ask me such a question. 'We spoke a couple of weeks ago, but she always calls me at intervals, so it's quite usual for me not to hear from her for a while.'

'I think you had better call someone, because I've heard she's been mugged.'

It seemed a very strange route for such personal information to reach me, but I was thankful that Peter called me and immediately tried to reach Mavis. There was no reply from her or other members of the family and I eventually decided to call the police near where Donna was living. They confirmed that she had been involved in an accident and suggested that I drive to Wythenshawe Hospital where she had been admitted.

This was no easy matter as Torquay was 250 miles and 4 hours journey time away. As I sat in the car, racing to see her, so many things rushed through my head. I didn't even have any hard information as to what had happened.

As I got nearer, I called the hospital and was advised that the press were gathering outside the main doors and so it was best to arrange a rendezvous nearby and then they could smuggle me in. I agreed because the last thing I wanted was to be faced with interviews and photos of me looking distressed at a time when all I wanted to do was see Donna.

I left my car with its personal plate tying it to me in a side road and an unmarked hospital car picked me up and drove me past more reporters and photographers than I could have imagined. As I crouched low in the back of the Mini, for some bizarre reason their presence reminded me of a crowd of red indians on the top of a hill waiting to commence battle. My heart sank at the thought that this was perhaps more serious than I had realized.

The driver whisked me round to a back door and took me into a quiet ward where the sister introduced herself.

'I'm afraid Donna isn't too well, but she's asleep at the moment.'

As I sat by Donna's bed, I was told that she had been horrifically attacked by a man friend who had been banned from seeing her by the police. Apparently he was leaving the country and telephoned to ask if he could see her one last time. She went to his flat where she was attacked from behind and left for dead.

I couldn't take any more. The sister could see that I was about to either faint or burst, so she led me to a small room by the swing doors of the ward. Once sat down, I began to cry.

'Why me, God?' I sobbed. 'Why Donna?'

After ten minutes and one of the sister's strong cups of tea, I returned to Donna. Standing there at her bedside, I couldn't imagine why anyone would want to hurt her. She couldn't speak and was barely awake, so, after a while, I left and headed for my sister Linda's house nearby.

I told Linda, who was also in a state of shock, that the prognosis from the medics wasn't good and that the next 24 hours would be crucial. I wanted to be near enough that I could be called back at a moment's notice. Mavis had also been to see Donna, so, when I arrived at Linda's house, I called her to get the full story as to why Donna was now fighting for her life.

After my time of listening and asking a thousand questions was over, I put the telephone down on Mavis in silence. I didn't know what to do next. I didn't feel like eating. I couldn't concentrate on a book, newspaper or television programme. I just felt awful and, above all, completely helpless. The motive for the attack was not known and I was told that the incident had now appeared in the press. The story was out, but at least I was now at her side. Following a short call to Sheree, I collapsed into bed. The day's events must have exhausted me to the bone because within minutes I was asleep.

I returned to the hospital the next day, where the nurse greeted me with a smile.

'She's out of intensive care today, Syd. She's on the mend!'

On hearing this, I could easily have kissed her, but just took her hand and shook it firmly instead.

When I began the slow journey back home, no one knew how fully her physical and mental scars would heal. How long would it take? Only time would tell. As my car raced along the M5, my mind was racing, too, with a million questions and some answers. I realized that I had already received an answer to my earlier, desperate prayer at the hospital.

'If you believe in God you have to believe in the devil,' I told myself. 'This wasn't God's work, this was from hell.'

'So why hadn't God stopped it? If he is a God of love as we are told, why could he not have prevented it?' asked the little devil on one shoulder.

'Because if God interrupted every bad thing that happens on this Earth, we would simply become his puppets,' I reasoned.

What I had to do now was trust God for the future and, as I headed westwards to Devon, that's exactly what I did. I placed Donna firmly in God's hands and I knew that it was the best and safest place she could be.

Over the long hot summer that followed, we slowly saw recovery take place, but I was still in shock about Paul. With Donna's attack happening so close to his funeral, I don't think that I had had enough time to grieve properly. There was certainly a process of recovery that needed to happen in me, too, and I was pleased that Little and Large were booked to appear at the Paradise Room on Blackpool's pleasure beach. I could work and be at home, too, and the timing of this reminded me that God's helping hand was still there.

Despite the fact that Paul had endured very deep mental and emotional problems, I still carried a certain amount of guilt around with me. Could I have done more to help? This constantly nagging question remained for years until, halfway through the season, Chris invited me to a comedians Bible study.

A lot of comedians were appearing in the roller-coaster town that summer and several turned up for the Bible study, very inquisitive to find out about these strange Christians who believed in God. Cannon and Ball were appearing at The Grand Theatre that summer and so, on the day, we met in Bobby and Tommy's dressing room.

Chris thought it was a good idea to bring us all together, but hadn't planned on a room full of comedians all cracking gags and trying to outdo each other. After half an hour of non-stop jokes, he eventually managed to get us all in order and the remaining 30 minutes were spent doing a backstage Bible study. Interestingly, the subject Chris chose was forgiveness. This is a crucial element of the gospel story and yet one that I had never quite grasped.

Chris explained that just knowing God isn't any help.

'Even the devil believes in God,' explained Chris. 'And if you look at the beautiful world around us, it's very hard to suppose we are all here by accident. I admire atheists, because with all this evidence of God on our doorsteps, I think they have a greater faith *not* to believe in God.'

Interesting.

'Neither does going to church make you a Christian any more than going to McDonalds makes you a hamburger!'

We comics tried not to laugh at Chris' attempts to be funny, even if they did make a good point. We didn't want to encourage him too much in this respect!

'You have to come and ask God to be in the driving seat of your life, and that's when he can really take over and steer you through the bad times.'

OK so far, I thought.

'One thing that God likes to do is to take away all the guilt that we carry by making so many mistakes in our lives. It's almost like we have to turn back the clock to when Adam and Eve told God that they could do without him. God let them go and the beautiful world that God had created became a terrible place to live because of mankind's selfishness and greed.'

I was beginning to understand.

'We made a complete mess of what God had intended, and now we have to say sorry.'

That made sense.

'But if we break the rules in our society, we have a price to pay. If I drive through a red traffic light today, the cost will either be that I shall be arrested by the police or, at worst, kill someone.'

I'm still with you.

'As God's own creation, there is nothing we can offer him that can repay this debt, so God sent Jesus to die in order to pay what we owe and wipe the slate clean.'

Now I understand.

'I've never asked God to forgive me,' I said shakily in front of all these comedians now looking straight at me. I knew some of them hadn't either, but I was too eager to get the guilt of Paul and other areas of my life off my back to worry about what they thought of me.

'All right, cock,' said Bobby in the wonderful way that he does. 'I'll say a prayer and you can just repeat after me.'

As I did so, the tears began to drop, then flow and finally gush. There were so many tears I wondered where they were all coming from – I didn't realize that I had so much water in me!

The tears continued and it felt like a whole well of fear, worry and guilt was being washed away from a river deep down inside. When I'd finished and stood up, I felt like a new person, like I had gone through a sort of spiritual MOT. My spark plugs had been replaced, the engine oil changed and I rushed to the theatre that night with a new spring in my step.

Eddie must have noticed something different because he looked at me and said, 'So where have you been?'

'Comedians Bible study,' said I.

Eddie – someone who wants to see the holes the nails made in Jesus' hands for himself before he will accept anything to do with God – was extremely sceptical. At least it opened up a conversation about spiritual things that continued on and off throughout the season. Sheree and her mum have always been churchgoers, so it was easy to share my newfound understanding of God with them.

As a youngster, I used to love going to church and particularly to see my Aunt Ethel for tea on a Sunday afternoon. Her house was full of pictures and one always used to catch my eye. It's the famous one of Jesus standing at the door and knocking, and I had kept this picture vividly in my mind since being a small boy.

When discussing this one day, Chris got a copy of it and pointed out that the door has no handle on the outside. Jesus could therefore only come into my life if I opened the door myself. This was exactly what I had done in Bobby and Tommy's dressing room and, now, the more I talked about God, the more I felt that I was getting to know him and he was certainly getting to know me.

'Good job,' I thought. 'After what has happened to me in the past few months, heaven only knows what'll be next!'

Heaven did know.

7

ANOTHER MARATHON

As if the traumas of Paul and Donna weren't enough, our poor son Dominic had also been going through a very tough time throughout this period.

As I mentioned earlier, Sheree and I refer to him as our miracle boy because when we got married we were told that we couldn't have children. After 13 years of marriage, we gave up trying and our little boy Dominic appeared!

Sadly, when he was just three years old, Dominic got pneumonia and the resulting long hospital ordeal involving needles and tubes upset him for life. He still shudders if he sees a needle, even if it's just on the television.

He then caught whooping cough when he was seven. Having recovered from this, a viral infection when he was 11 set the scene for a new problem. He had just gone up into what they called the middle school at Rossall and was excited about leaving junior school behind him. He found the change quite stressful, though, and had to spend much time proving himself academically. All this made him quite low, which is how we think this viral infection caught hold.

Dominic had been like me – like a piece of streaky bacon, but healthy with it. The infection lasted a couple of weeks and kept him in bed with flu-like symptoms. It left an imprint on his immune system that slowly took away everything that seemed necessary to keep him alive.

A schoolteacher came up to Sheree one day and said:

'What's wrong with Dominic? He looks like a little old man walking across the playground with his books.'

A few days later, Sheree got a call from the school.

'I think you need to come and take Dominic home,' said the voice. 'He can't seem to move out of his chair.'

When Sheree picked him up that afternoon, he was so exhausted that she took him home and he went straight to bed. He still went in to school the next day, but Sheree had to pick him up again before the day was through.

After this, things just started to get worse. There were days when Dominic couldn't even get out of bed because of an acute lack of energy. He often lay in bed all day awake. For someone who hates being in bed, this was torture for him. Friends came round to see him as much as possible, but often he was too fatigued to join in. When he did get up, he crawled along the floor and down the stairs on his bottom and sometimes he was too weak to stand up.

Dominic's house master suggested that it could be ME – something that we had heard of, but knew very little about. After conversations with other parents and friends, together with books and articles Sheree read, we were pretty convinced that the diagnosis was indeed ME, or myalgic encephalitis.

By this time, Sheree and I were very worried and she took him to a local doctor.

'I had to carry him into the surgery, Syd,' she told me on the mobile that morning. I knew that Dominic's weight had dropped dramatically to four stone and he had simply collapsed on to the floor one day, unable to stand unaided any more. Carrying him up the stairs and down the stairs was easy because he was so light.

'I would have carried him whatever weight he was,' Sheree had said to me. 'It's not a burden, just something that needs to be done.' I thought she was being incredibly brave. I was feeling terrible because I was away a lot and had to leave

Sheree to deal with it all. At least we were in constant contact on the mobile.

'The GP was wonderfully supportive and confirmed that it probably was ME, but it could also be rheumatoid arthritis, which would explain the dramatic weight loss,' Sheree explained to me on the phone. I was relieved to hear that at last there was some progress in finding an explanation for Dominic's suffering.

After several blood tests, it was confirmed that he did indeed have ME, also known as chronic fatigue syndrome (CFS). It may also be called post-viral fatigue syndrome (PVFS). It is pretty common among teenagers, particularly girls. The illness seems to be more common in young people aged between 13 and 15, but children as young as 5 can also be affected. Stress, from exams or peer competition, can play a part in triggering it, as can some sort of trauma. The younger you are, the easier it is to get rid of, we heard. There was no specific treatment, but getting the right information early on would help Dominic manage the illness and give him the best chance of recovery.

The illness can begin as long ago as ten years before it is diagnosed and affects many parts of the body, such as the nervous and immune systems. The most common symptoms are severe fatigue or exhaustion, problems with memory and concentration and muscle pain. These were all things that Dominic regularly complained about.

It has been estimated that there are up to 240,000 people with ME in the UK, of which around 25,000 are children and young people. It can also affect men and women from all social and ethnic groups. It seems to be more common to develop the illness between your early twenties and mid-forties.

The disease used to be nicknamed the yuppie disease because it was not considered to be a genuine disorder, but more of a psychological one. Now it is recognized as being a very real problem, but more research is needed before these abnormalities and their impact are properly understood.

We were also warned that it was time that would be the healer, as his body made its own slow recovery, but it could still take several years.

'The doctor said that he'll get through this eventually,' Sheree continued to explain. 'It just needs time.'

Sheree said that she thanked the doctor for all her help and I thanked Sheree for gathering all the information. At least we knew as much as possible to help Dominic fight this dreadful problem, even though he was displaying six out of the seven symptoms of this disease.

One thing that I found hard to take was seeing him suffer so much. I could hear his bones creak. When Sheree was on the telephone to Dominic's godmother, she said:

'What's that horrible noise in the background?'

'Oh, that's Dominic groaning with the pain in his muscles,' she replied.

By this time, we had to investigate the possibility of hiring a wheelchair from the NHS because Dominic was unable to walk alone. This prospect was the last thing we wanted for Dominic. He just seemed to be getting worse and a wheelchair felt like the final acknowledgement of this.

'He could be in this for life,' I said to Sheree as we folded and packed the apparatus in the car boot one day and took it home. When Charlie, a friend who was suffering from cerebral palsy, offered to lend us a wheelchair he no longer used, we were really grateful.

Charlie had recently been thrown out of a shopping centre by an ignorant security guard who didn't realize that he had CP and assumed he was drunk. We were to have our own interesting moments in the street with Dominic. I was to discover just how difficult it is to shunt a heavy wheelchair up and down over kerbs and so on and I now have every sympathy with wheelchair users.

We attracted people's attention anyway because we were with a wheelchair, but even more so because I am well known. Some people came up to me and were unable to understand why Dominic couldn't walk. To anybody who suggested to me when I explained that it was not a proper condition, and just a con, I would say:

'What 12-year-old boy do you know would *choose* to spend his life in a wheelchair?'

I was amazed when one of the most negative comments turned out to be from a specialist we had taken Dominic to see for a check-up:

'There's nothing wrong with him,' said the specialist. 'I want to see you come back here next week with some dirt on your trainers, young lad!'

He was very dismissive, but we knew instinctively that there was nothing being faked here, this was for real.

Christmas and birthday presents for Dominic that year consisted of PC games and Lego – things that didn't use up too much energy.

Over the following weeks, things got worse and worse. Sheree's Mum and Dad would look after him while Sheree and I worked, but Sheree was on the phone every hour or so to see if Dominic was OK.

'Feed him up', was the advice of the doctors, but it's useless if your patient just doesn't have the energy to put anything in to his stomach. His weight loss was such that he looked like a skeleton.

It wasn't long before the GP came round to inspect Dominic again and immediately requested that he be admitted to hospital. The GP wasn't happy at all and thought that he should be closely monitored.

At this point, our hearts sank to their lowest point. Here was our emaciated son, literally dying in front of us and there was nothing we could do. We even began to think that the problem was deeper than ME. Perhaps it was cancer?

Even Dominic lost hope.

'What's the point?' he said.

Sheree and I felt hopeless, too. We sat on the edge of Dominic's hospital bed and prayed the most simple, but perhaps the most effective, prayer there is:

'Please help us Lord!'

We were always a close couple, despite my strange working hours and odd career. In spite of the media pressure and inability to be at home for those special occasions, we were still each other's best friend. The problems with Paul and Donna had brought us even closer together and I knew that the trauma we now faced with Dominic would do the same.

'Everything we have gone through, we have gone through together,' said Sheree as we held hands. 'This is no different.'

I still had to work. I still had to go out and make people laugh, even though at the back of my mind was the worry of how Dominic was and how Sheree was coping. We rang each other a lot on the mobile. How I would have coped without that little machine I just don't know. We could laugh together and cry together even if I was on the opposite side of the country – sometimes I was on the opposite side of the world.

Sheree stayed at the hospital with Dominic for nearly a week. I popped in and out and sat with them both during the day as much as I could.

When he got back home, things seemed to take a turn for the better. Whether this was as a result of our prayers or Dominic's determination to get better or a bit of both I just don't know. What I do know is that what I call God-incidents always seem to happen when I put things in God's hands.

'I'm not going to be like this, Mum,' Dominic announced to Sheree one morning as he struggled to pull himself out of bed unaided. His sense of motivation was so unexpected.

Initially we were worried because we didn't want him to overdo things and make his prognosis worse. On the other hand, we didn't want to squash his inner strength and resolve to win through. We still worried. Were we being overprotective? What was the right and best thing to do? No one had the answers; we just had to take each day at a time.

I knew that there was a bit in the Bible about not worrying about tomorrow because today has enough worries of its own. I've always thought that this is good advice and now put it into practice in the most obvious way. As Dominic made a painfully slow recovery, we could see that at last there was light at the end of the tunnel and we just kept our focus on going forwards towards it.

He soon requested to go back to school. After several months of being at home, Dominic decided that he could no longer afford to miss any more school. He was particularly worried about being put back a year and then having to spend another 12 months catching up. He had kept going with plenty of homework, but it wasn't the same as being at the school that he enjoyed so much.

Most people were very supportive of the idea – none more so than the staff and pupils at his school, in spite of the difficulties of manoeuvring a wheelchair around. At first, Sheree would take Dominic to school and would then return at intervals throughout the day to transport him from one classroom to another. It was hard work getting the chair up and down the spiral staircase as there were no lifts in the old school building. It was exhausting for Sheree, but she was very committed to helping Dominic as much as possible. After a while, though, both teachers and pupils offered to help.

'You don't need to come in every day,' they said. 'We'll look after him.'

Apparently they had some fun and were all jumping on the chair for free rides. The pupils, I mean, not the teachers! It was good to see some laughter in among the sadness of it all. There were a few occasions, too, when I was doing some gospel gigs and Chris pulled together a few ministers and other church folk together in a room to specifically put Dominic and us, his family, into God's hands. I do believe in the power of prayer and this and being back at school seemed to have a positive effect on Dominic.

After a few months, Dominic started to improve even more and started to wheel himself over to Farmer Parr's Animal World, just up the road from us. Farmer Parr had obviously seen how fed up Dominic was looking about still being in a wheelchair and how frustrated he was that he couldn't help out with all the fun that was going on.

'Look what I've found, Dominic – a pair of crutches,' Farmer Parr said to him one day. 'Why not have a go with them and see how you get on?'

With the farmer's help, Dominic eased himself out of the wheelchair and started walking with the crutches. He had been in the wheelchair for 14 months before this moment of being able to transfer to using crutches. From that day on, Dominic decided to use the crutches as much as possible, but we still wondered if he would make it or collapse again. Is this too early? We questioned everything again.

When we saw that he was coping more and more ably with the crutches and even giving us the occasional triumphant smile, it was a huge encouragement. The light at the end of the tunnel was getting brighter at last.

The decision to take an autumn holiday with his mother and grandmother in the South of France wasn't taken lightly either, but it seemed the next logical step in his recovery. It did him the world of good, the sunshine and fresh air bringing their own healing.

Sheree rang me from France one day and told me that Dominic had been sitting in the garden when he suddenly gave her a very defiant look.

'Syd, he's off his crutches! He's walking on his own today!'

I sat in the car and wept, then looked up at the blue sky and said a quiet 'Thank you'.

Holidays have become a big part of our family life now. Whether a long weekend break or an extended trip abroad, we know how important it is to get away and have time for each other. The problem is that being in the entertainment industry has meant that I am often performing when everybody else is resting. When I'm off, Dominic is back at school and Sheree is working, so we have to be very clever about how we snatch time away. The pressure, pace and unsocial hours of my work mean that it is more important than ever for us to take family holidays as regularly as possible. One day I was reading my Bible and realized that even Jesus had to take a break away from it all and go out into the middle of the lake. If he needed it, how much more do I!

It wasn't always like this, though. In the early days of Little and Large I just worked non-stop because I always expected my career to come to an abrupt end. It was obvious that I should take the work while I could. When the pace refused to wane, though, it was our agent then, Norman Murray, who suggested that we take time off. We'd just done a long summer season in Blackpool, immediately followed by a long pantomime engagement at the Liverpool Empire and then straight into another summer season at the Britannia Pier in Great Yarmouth. It had become usual for my diary to be booked up three years in advance like this and, in those days, one season ran into another. With no end in sight before our next pantomime in Oxford, I got a call from Norman one day:

'I've cleared a three-week break in your diary after February,' he explained.

'What for?' I said, not a little nervously, thinking that I had done something wrong.

'You need a break,' he said. 'Make sure you take one!'

Sheree was thrilled at the prospect when I told her of course and we spent many hours on the telephone in the following months swapping ideas about where to go. We tried to imagine the most luxurious place on Earth, a place where we would pamper ourselves. So it was that our first ever proper holiday was to Barbados. A spectacular place and, ironically, also one of the most theatrical.

I had never been on anything bigger than a private plane before, so when I climbed abroad the gleaming white jumbo jet, I was incredulous at the amount of space there was before me. It seemed like there were seats stretching for miles and I wondered if the trip was into outer space rather than just the Caribbean.

'This thing will never get off the ground!' I said to Sheree, who had some cajoling to do before she finally persuaded me to stay put.

Having held tightly on to the arms of the seat during take-off, I was soon recognized by one of the stewardesses, who asked me if I would like to meet the captain. I thought he was going to pop out and shake hands, but, instead, I was ushered out of my seat and into the cockpit, which was the biggest contrast to the rest of the plane I could ever have imagined. Even little me felt huge inside this tiny metal cabin bursting with dials, controls and switches. I had to duck my head down to avoid hitting anything I shouldn't. I was desperate to steer clear of accidentally pressing something with my elbow that would send the plane into an immediate dive.

I asked a few questions and wanted to know what some of the buttons and levers did, but the captain and his crew seemed more interested in having a celebrity aboard their plane.

'It's great to see you, Syd. We've watched your programmes for what seems like forever!'

I received his words graciously and his comments about having seen me on telly 'forever' helped to remind me why I was actually on the plane. A holiday was definitely needed.

'Well, if having a celebrity aboard makes them take extra

care on landing, then that's fine by me!' I smiled at Sheree as I slipped my way gingerly back into my seat.

It wasn't long before a meal was served, but no sooner had I got my tray of food on the table in front of me than the warning lights began flashing on and off.

'Ladies and gentlemen, we are expecting a little bit of turbulence in the next few minutes and I advise you to ensure that your seatbelts are securely fastened,' came the captain's voice over the public address system.

Up until then, the ride had been as smooth as anything, but now, with my dinner in front of me and a glass of red wine in my hand, it became like a scene from *It's a Knockout*. This popular programme on Friday nights featured teams of unwitting contestants who battled against the greatest odds to play the weirdest games imaginable. Trying to get as much chicken and vegetables in my mouth as possible while preventing my wine from filling someone else's glass suddenly became a full-time occupation. I'm sure I could have won this heat if it had been one of the games played on the TV show.

I had just managed to finish a final mouthful of trifle and let out a triumphant 'yes' in Sheree's direction when the seatbelt lights went out and all was horizontal again.

'Was that some sort of heavenly joke?' I asked my wife.

When the plane landed, I was first at the door to get out. After nine hours, I was feeling a little claustrophobic and my knees were aching. When I climbed down the metal stairs holding Sheree's hand, the heat that hit us was tremendous. It was as if the angels had turned on a giant hairdryer right in our faces. It took several days to get used to the intensity of it.

The first few days of settling in were pretty hectic, as we darted here and there, until I suddenly realized that everybody else was walking ten times slower than us. We had worked hard for two years non-stop and it was only after not working for a few days that it dawned on me just how manic the pace of my life was. Now enjoying the heat of the famed west coast of Barbados, the gentleness of the waves creeping up the white sandy shore near the Coral Reef Hotel with its quiet atmosphere and 12 acres of beautiful landscaped gardens full of tropical flowers and mature trees, I was finally coaxed, and cooked, into calm submission. By midweek, I could be seen sitting down reading a newspaper, even if it was a few days out of date. We could also choose from golf, sailing, skiing, windsurfing or snorkelling at the underwater park just adjacent to the hotel, but our days were mainly filled with relaxation and quiet strolls along the unbroken expanse of the beach. The restaurant overlooked the calm Caribbean Sea and it was great to be able to have a chance to talk to Sheree face to face rather than with a telephone in my hand and put my clothes in a wardrobe instead of living out of a suitcase all the time.

For over 40 years the O'Hara family have provided the warm hospitality and impeccable service for which the Coral Reef Club is so famous and we were really well looked after. As we sat sipping cocktails on the beach, we knew that this was as close to the perfect holiday as we would ever find.

One of the problems of being well known is being spotted by someone when I'm trying to relax. I realize that I owe my career to the public so, most of the time, I don't mind. It's a bit odd, though, when someone wants to take a picture of me and I'm just wearing my swimming shorts or they stare for ages and then come up and say, 'Are you who I think you are?'

'That depends on who you think I am!' I reply.

Another sunny day on the beach, I was being looked at by someone I presumed was a fan of Little and Large. It turned out that he wasn't staring because of the TV series, but because I was wearing a pair of swimming shorts on my head! I was taking the locals' advice to keep out of the sun and it seemed sensible to me to make sure that my head was covered with the most suitable bit of cloth I could find. The shorts fitted round my head perfectly, but it was unlikely that this would become a new beach fashion. With the two legs of the shorts sticking up in the air, it must have looked like I was growing horns, so it was no wonder that the little boy was laughing out loud.

Eventually the boy's father came over to see what all the fuss was about and immediately knew who I was. He must have assumed that I was wearing the shorts on my head to amuse his son, because he beamed with a sort of appreciative smile as he said:

'Hi, Syd! I knew it must have been someone in show-business making my boy laugh so much.'

I smiled back weakly.

'Where are you working next summer?' he asked, which was a question I wasn't prepared for.

'Bournemouth,' I replied confidently.

'Great, I'll send some of my goods round.' Then he was gone. Sheree and I wondered what on Earth these 'goods' were and hoped they weren't something that would get me bad press in the papers again!

It soon became obvious that others from the business had also discovered the tranquillity that Barbados had to offer. I had not realized that the island was such a celebrity hotspot. Whenever we went out, we seemed to bump into people we knew. Hiding in a corner of the hotel bar one day we found Gilbert O'Sullivan, known for several pop hits, including the famous 'Clair' and 'Alone Again (Naturally)'.

I kept my distance for a while in case he'd wanted some privacy. Then I, literally, bumped into him while trying to order some drinks. Apparently he was staying at the hotel for a few weeks while his agents and managers took another look at his career to make decisions and suggestions as to which way he should go. After a long career in the pop world with a string of hits to your name, it's often difficult to know what to do next, he explained to us. I could relate to this, and the question of how long the Little and Large phenomenon would last before we were replaced by someone or something else had crossed my mind.

We got on really well with Gilbert and his wife and shared many a drink together without it feeling as if we were back on the showbiz circuit or that there was any danger of Sheree telling me off for talking business on holiday. In fact, it was Gilbert who told Sheree off one day.

'Your nose is too red!' he announced over a drink one evening. 'You must be careful not to stay in the sun for too long.'

I'm sure it was Gilbert's advice that kept us from suffering from sunstroke, even though we went on a very long boat trip around the island halfway through our stay. It was the 'Jolly Roger Cruise' and it certainly lived up to its name. Playing silly games in the water was just up my street. Sheree meanwhile got chatting to a lady in the ship's lounge and sensed that they had much in common. She explained that she was on holiday with her husband and that he was sitting in a chair over on the other side of the boat. When Sheree pointed him out to me, I recognized the figure wearing a panama and sitting in the shade away from the sun and the crowd as Peter Skellern. Composer, singer and musician Peter shot to fame with his UK top three hit, the ballad 'You're a Lady', which he wrote while working as a hotel porter in Shaftesbury, Dorset. As a result, he could now afford to stay in a different sort of hotel. Another hit – 'Love is the Sweetest Thing' – in 1979 won him a Music Trades Association Award for Best MOR album.

Peter's albums reflected the breadth of his musical interests, from ballads to ragtime, with folk traditions. He was an expert at witty, yet homely, love songs, such as 'Hold on to Love', which were written in the Gilbert O'Sullivan style. When I approached him later to say a quick hello, he was very pleased to see us, but wasn't at all keen to meet Gilbert O'Sullivan, who, as we've seen, was staying at our hotel. I thought this was a bit strange at first, but, after some time chatting, I realized just how shy Peter really was. In fact, Gilbert O'Sullivan was just as shy and I wondered if the fact that they were both pianists had anything to do with it. So, although they were both staying in the same resort, they never met and I never got a chance to be a professional matchmaker as it were. Perhaps they have met since.

After two weeks, it was time to go home and get back to work, but holidays remained a key part of our life as a family. Not much later, we took Dominic on holiday to the US of A.

Dad was mad keen on Mickey Mouse and collected as many souvenirs as he could. He had a whole range of pictures, postcards and badges, as well as some little toys that stood on the mantelpiece at home. Mum said that whenever he was away from home, he would always sketch a Disney character on the postcards he sent her.

When I was small, I was proud that we had wallpaper with all the Disney characters smiling and laughing as they looked down upon us. This wasn't purchased in a shop, but painstakingly handpainted on the walls by Dad. In my bedroom was Pinocchio sitting on a bench in Gepetto's shop with the blue fairy waving her wand over him to bring him alive. It was a magical scene to wake up to each morning.

My brother had a picture of the sandman, who throws sand in children's eyes to help them go to sleep, against a background of strange-looking trees with faces and arms stretching across the wall.

Even in Mum and Dad's bedroom, there was a painting of a huge mountain with a lake in front of it instead of a bedhead. Around the window stretched trees and ivy, which made it look like you were outside the house rather than inside it.

When Granada Television invited me back to walk along Moorcroft Road, Wythenshawe, for a documentary, to talk about my old childhood haunts, it was like going back in time. As we were filming, about 50 rough-looking kids suddenly appeared from nowhere. From the age of six upwards, they all seemed to be puffing away on cigarettes as they watched us. Apparently these kids were so difficult to manage that they had even caused my old local church, St Michael's and All Angels, to close because they kept running in and out and disrupting the services.

'Are you famous, mister?' said one with the scruffiest hair I had ever seen.

'Well, I used to live in that house over there,' I gestured.

'Oh yeah,' he said in a strangely knowledgeable way. 'That's the one with all those pictures on the wall, ain't it?'

I was absolutely dumbstruck, realizing that not only did this little boy know all about the cartoons, but also they were still there all these years later. Due to the codes of conduct for filming, we weren't allowed to knock on the door unannounced, though I would have loved to have seen those cartoons again.

So, when we went to Disneyland, it was like a dream come true and it was in some strange way like I was doing it for Dad. When we first arrived and saw the beauty of Cinderella's castle, I was immediately transported back to the elegance of the film and felt just like a prince with my princess as I walked down the stairs hand in hand with Sheree while 'When you wish upon a star . . .' played in the background. Ahh! It was all so romantic . . .

We couldn't resist going on all the rides at Disneyland, including the one called '20,000 Leagues Under the Sea' aboard the *Nautilus* submarine. It's gone now I think, but, at the time, when I sat aboard the submarine, it really did feel like we were going deeper and deeper in, then round the lagoon. Looking through the window, I was terrified at the sight of a huge, tentacled octopus approaching us fast. Only at the last moment did it divert itself away, but I'm sure that it gave me a wink as it did so!

'Pirates of the Caribbean' proved to be my favourite ride. I'm not one for fast and furious roller-coasters – I prefer something with a scene to enjoy. With words like 'Dead men tell no tales', 'Ye come seeking adventure and salty pirates? Aye, this be the place . . .' and promises that a trip through the 'Pirates of the Caribbean' will allow guests to 'set sail with the wildest crew that ever sacked the Spanish Main!' plastered all over the walls as we queued to get in, I was already in the mood.

Not only did this ride take us on a fantasy journey around the sea and coastline of the Caribbean, but there was plenty of comedy, too. After climbing in to our boat, it drifted off through the mist under a very realistic moonlit night sky. The sounds of crickets, frogs, toads and alligators could be heard as we drifted slowly towards the stone walls of a canal, which then swept us quickly towards a dark corridor. Before long, the relative quiet of the swamp erupted into a loud, rollicking adventure on all sides as the pirates, in all their glory, sang their songs and shot their cannons right over our heads! I ducked down several times in the boat, despite Sheree glaring at me for behaving like a little boy. Surely not? I've been back to this ride several times now and, on each visit, I still want to jump out of the boat and join in the fun going on ashore, but I shall have to do it when Sheree isn't with me!

Many different types of holiday followed and it still amazes me who I meet on the way. A couple of years ago, I bumped into Timothy Spall, of *Auf Wiedersehen, Pet* fame and for appearing in numerous other TV series and films. When I started talking to him, I was so surprised at how posh he sounded after hearing his Barry character's Brummie accent that he used in the series. Perhaps I had momentarily forgotten that he was an actor and a very good one, too. So I safely assumed, correctly as it turned out, that his character in the Harry Potter film *Harry Potter and the Prisoner of Azkaban* wouldn't have a Brummie accent either.

Madeira was a lovely island, but there didn't seem a lot to do, so we took a long walk one day and ended up in what seemed to be a very derelict area. Right in the middle of all this was the most beautiful restaurant. It was called the Golfina and, as I stepped inside, I thought for a moment that I was back aboard the *Nautilus* again as I was surrounded by brass portholes and huge iron doors. It was just like a ship, so I wasn't that surprised to discover that it was full of sailors. The amazing thing, though, was that it was full of British sailors. In fact, they were the crew of HMS *Phoebe* and, having seen at sea for eight months, had been given shore leave by the captain.

'Fancy seeing you here of all places,' they said, and I felt the same way about them too. Of all the days we decided to take a walk.

'Why not pop aboard tomorrow?' they said. 'We're docked not far from here. No one on board will believe we've met you if you don't.'

How could we refuse? At 12.20 precisely the next day, we climbed slowly up the gangplank and were taken to an officer's mess where plenty of drink and some pretty tasty morsels were on offer. After a while, a strange naval ritual involving a request from another petty officer to transfer us to a different mess began to unfold. We went from one mess to another like this and, by the end of all the drinking and talking, I really was in a bit of a fine mess myself. Sheree and I tipsily wobbled back down the gangplank at nearly 7 p.m. and, having got back to the hotel, slept right through till the following morning.

Now, at the time of writing, I am about to take yet another holiday. This time it's off to a friend's caravan in Silloth, about 20 miles from Carlisle, in the middle of nowhere. Well, it's nice to have a change from Barbados!

It took three years – from the ages of 11 to 13 – for Dominic's body to finally beat the virus and his immune system to properly repair itself. When I talked a little about Dominic's ME during my interview with Chris at a gospel gig in Welling one night in 2003, I announced:

'Yesterday, he ran the school marathon – 1500 metres cross-country – and came twenty-fourth out of 158. Not bad, eh?'

There was a big round of applause. As I had told them the whole story in a nutshell, it must have seemed like a biblical miracle to the audience. In fact, Dominic went on to swim for his house and was even mentioned during the principal's address on speech day:

'Rossall School has the true spirit to get us all through. This is shown no better than in the way that Dominic has fought through his illness and come out the other side.'

The virus is still in his body, but Dominic knows that he must manage his time and effort properly in order to prevent it from taking over his system again. The illness has meant that he's had to grow up an awful lot more quickly than his friends and he's now a fully fledged teenager who eats like a horse. There is no need to go back to the doctor – he just takes some painkillers if he ever has a day when he feels a bit under par. We can be at a party one evening and he will turn to us and say, 'I need to go home.'

Needless to say, we are very proud of him.

Now, after his sessions on the rowing machine in his bedroom, which have made his muscles stronger, he can easily beat me up, so I have to be careful what I say these days! He's gone from size six shoes to size nine in two years and I'm disappointed because I can't wear his cast-offs any more!

In February 2003, it was announced that clinical guidelines for the diagnosis and treatment of CFS/ME were to be developed by the National Institute of Clinical Excellence (NICE). Clinical guidelines are the latest step in the Department of Health's strategy to improve the care given to people with ME. Plans for clinical network centres and teams across England were announced in January 2004. Sheree, Dominic and I welcome any steps that are being taken to bring help to those suffering from this dreadful illness in the way that we have as a family.

Chris Clark, chief executive of Action for ME – an organization that provides information, help and support for sufferers – said that:

'Many people with ME have really struggled even to get a diagnosis. We welcome the long-awaited news of NICE guidelines and hope they will equip health professionals to provide better care for people with ME.'

Sheree and I would advise parents whose child has just been diagnosed to never give up hope. 'God doesn't put us in bubble wrap,' said Sheree to me one day as we sat watching Dominic working at Farmer Parr's, looking just like any other normal teenager. 'We all walk the same path, but our faith means that God walks with us. We are never alone and that's the difference.' She's right of course. Time heals, but we live in an instant world where we want instant cures. In Dominic's case, we needed patience, strength and the kind of hope that, we believe, could only have come from a heavenly source. We could never have got through it all without it.

As for holidays that help to bring healing, a few weeks after getting back home from Madeira, a letter was handed to me backstage just before a show. 'Dear Syd,' it said. 'We are all in the audience tonight as our ship just docked at Plymouth and we have driven over to see you so that you can make us all laugh.' It was signed by the crew of HMS *Phoebe* and I will never forget the fun and laughter I had leaving the stage door that night surrounded by these sailors.

Nor will I forget that, a few weeks after our Barbados

holiday, a huge box like a tea chest turned up at the stage door during our summer season in Bournemouth.

'I think it's for you, Syd,' said the stage door keeper, looking at me in a very suspicious manner.

'Really? Is it ticking?' I asked.

As I opened the lid, I gasped in amazement, for it was crammed full of packets of popcorn. Among the packaging was a note from the man we had met on the beach when I was wearing my swimming shorts on my head. He was the head of the Butterkist popcorn firm and he was keeping his promise to send me some 'goods'. The popcorn lasted me, my family and friends for months, but the happy memories of being on holiday with my family and seeing Dominic well again will last forever.

8

TAKING BUDDY HOLLY
TO CHURCH

It was in Swansea in 1996 that Chris Gidney popped in to see me during one of his marathon countryside panto cast visits. Somehow, Chris manages to reach around 15 panto casts a year, travelling all over the country, offering support and encouragement as he goes. He believes that the skills involved in comedy, music, dance and the magic of theatre are God-given ones and is keen to make sure that performers know God cares about them.

Chris wanted to ensure that I knew this, too, but I noticed a different kind of twinkle in his eye as he walked in and sat down on the red sofa.

'Syd, have you thought of doing some solo work?'

I was astounded.

'What do you mean?' is all I could offer. 'I've been a double act for nearly 35 years, how can I ever perform alone now?'

'I think God wants you to know how much he values you as an individual, as well as part of a double act,' said Chris, looking straight at me.

He was serious in a way that I hadn't seen before. Despite being what I call a travelling vicar (a title he hates so much that I love winding him up about it), he's not in any way a 'Bible-basher' and is normally very light, funny and easy to talk to. Now he was deadly serious, though, and this was a conversation he obviously wasn't prepared to have me discuss too quickly.

A whole clump of excuses suddenly came to my mind. What would I do? Where would I work? What would Eddie think? It was because of Chris' own experience, gained by working on and producing various shows, that I was prepared to listen just a little bit longer.

'Why don't we do a few gigs in some churches as a trial?' Chris had obviously thought this through during his journey along the M4 – more so than I had anticipated. I was both intrigued and terrified at the prospect at the same time.

'I'll introduce you. You can sing a song and then I'll interview you,' he offered.

Put that way, it didn't sound too bad, but I knew it wasn't exactly a usual career move. When I mentioned it to Sheree, she was surprisingly positive about the idea. It was all a bit unknown, but secretly I liked the idea of doing something on my own for a change. After all, Eddie did his after-dinner speaking, so maybe it was my turn. If I failed miserably, at least it wouldn't be in front of thousands, I thought. Surely, though, no one would be interested in seeing just one part of a double act – I wasn't even the funniest half.

When Chris introduced me to Dave Bemment, who was looking after the diaries and booking several of Chris' contacts in the business at that time, I knew it was all for real. Now I really did have to get my act together, literally.

'Why not start with a Buddy Holly medley?' suggested Chris as we talked it all through one day while travelling in my car. I was so taken aback that I swerved and nearly hit one of the Blackpool trams running by the side of the road.

'You can't be serious? Buddy Holly in church?!'

I thought that churches were places to be serious in, not have fun and a laugh and certainly not to sing rock 'n' roll.

Somehow Chris persuaded me that most churchgoers love music of all kinds and would not hold it against me. We eventually agreed on a menu of Buddy Holly, Gene Pitney, Robbie Williams and Boyzone! I was convinced that I would shock the few little old ladies with long faces sparsely arranged in the pews into walking out on me.

Imagine my own shock when I arrived in Eaglescliffe on the first date of a mini-tour to see a huge modern church, complete with dining rooms, kitchens and even an indoor football pitch.

'We like to offer something to our community,' said the minister as he showed me round the amazing new complex.

When we got into the main hall, I couldn't believe it. There were no pews. Only seats – 1500 of them. They looked comfortable, too.

'How embarrassing,' I thought. 'A huge venue like this and I'll just be playing to the front row.'

'We've sold out, by the way,' came the minister's voice, as if he had heard and was now answering my thoughts.

I really couldn't believe what I was seeing or hearing.

'Who's on then?' I quipped.

'You are!' he said.

Two hours and a sound check later, I was standing at the side of the triangular stage watching the support act Juliet Dawn sing through the lights and smoke a selection of Abba material. I could hear the audience singing and clapping along and I had to pinch myself twice. First, because it all felt like a bit of a dream and, second, because I wanted to know how on Earth Chris had managed to talk me into doing something so bizarre.

As I watched at the side of the stage, I gingerly peeped out into the audience. All the people seemed to be having a great time, laughing and clapping, yet what amazed me was that this was not happening in a theatre, but in a church! My preconceptions of church life and Christians being irrelevant, dead and boring began crossing my mind. I'd been a church-goer for most of my life, but I'd never seen anything like this on a Sunday.

Suddenly, once again, I felt like a fish out of the water as here I was, dressed in my blue rock 'n' roll Teddy boy costume, about to go on a stage and sing a Buddy Holly medley. In a church! The last time I had worn this costume was in Blackpool, starring with Eddie in our show 'Rock with Laughter' at the Grand Theatre. I really couldn't believe what I was doing wearing this sort of gear in such a holy place and I was about to go out on my own for the first time in 34 years.

Suddenly Chris bounced on stage and threw a few gags at the audience to warm them up. They started to laugh (even at Chris' jokes!), but it didn't put me at my ease at all. All I could think about was facing an audience completely alone. There was no one else to hold on to, either physically, comically or emotionally. It was just me. Whatever I said would not be enhanced by anyone else because there was only me. What would they think? What would they expect?

My teeth then started to chatter. This was something that, in all the years of stressful performances in front of millions, even the Queen, I had never experienced. Then my knees joined in. It was as if my teeth and knees were both engaged in beating time to one of the songs I was about to sing. They were knocking so hard together it was actually hurting me.

Then all too soon I heard the words:

'And now, ladies and gentlemen, will you give a warm welcome to your star guest for tonight . . . Mr Syd Little!'

At that moment my legs completely gave way under me. I had difficulty climbing on to the stage, but, when I did, the warmth of the audience hit me and the applause increased in the most reassuring way.

'Good evening,' I started, surprised that I was able to talk at all. 'My name's Syd Little and I'm going to start off by singing some old Buddy Holly songs, because there aren't any new ones!'

It got a big laugh, even though it seemed cheeky to not

only rock 'n' roll in a church but also make them giggle as well. The band struck up and I was on a roll. The Buddy Holly medley finished with a bit that the audience could join in with and, at the end, the whole crowd of 1500 people were singing along as if it were some sort of posh football match.

My spot finished with a big round of applause and I undid my guitar strap to put the guitar back on its rest. I discovered that my hands were shaking so much that I couldn't control the guitar enough to put it on to its holder. Fortunately, Chris came bounding on and rescued me by taking it off my hands and inviting me to sit down for a chat. The next 20 minutes were some of the happiest I had ever experienced on stage. Chris, the gentle question master, guided me through a whole catalogue of professional events, from things that had gone wrong on stage to meeting the Queen.

'The first time we met the Queen, Eddie showed me up,' I responded. 'We'd only ever seen her on a stamp before, so when we met her he licked the side of her face!'

There were plenty of these gags dotted through our chat about life in showbusiness and, then, after another couple of songs, Chris asked if we could talk about my personal life. I thought this would be difficult as I had never actually talked about what had happened to Paul and Donna in public before.

Amazingly, the words seemed to flow pretty easily, but I got a little choked at one point, talking about how Paul had died, and could hear the gasps from the audience when I mentioned what Donna had been through. The audience listened intently throughout and I wondered for a moment if they had drifted off to sleep.

My tragic personal story does have a happy ending, though, and it was good to come back to laughter and applause at the end when I talked about Donna and Dominic getting better. Then I sang a song to finish where I explained how, no matter what happens, God is always there to help if we let him, and I introduced it like this:

'This is a song recorded by a band called Boyzone. Well, I'm Boys-one!'

Afterwards, it was as if a huge burden had been lifted off me – the same sort of feeling you have when you talk about a problem to an understanding friend. It all felt quite therapeutic and I was happy to chat to people afterwards and sign a few autographs. Many people said how much they had enjoyed it and some related similar stories of sons or daughters who had been on drugs or alcohol.

It was such an encouraging evening all round that when Chris asked me if I would like to do some more, I jumped at the opportunity and I've made space in my professional diary to do so ever since. Nick Page runs an organization called Shorehill Arts and now looks after all my gospel bookings. He's very thorough and I appreciate that, because sometimes I need looking after. I'm not a businessman, an accountant or an agent, just a 'turn'. My job is to entertain people, so I leave the administration to Nick and he has been a great support.

'I would love to be on that programme *Celebrity Stars in Their Eyes*,' I said to Chris on stage one day. 'I do a fantastic Gene Pitney.'

'Was she a good singer?' asked Chris.

'Not *Jean*, *Gene*,' I explained. Oh, the uninitiated!

Chris asked the audience if they would like to see me do my impression and, as they said they would, I launched into the vocally stressful song 'I'm Gonna be Strong' with a very high note to hit at the end. Somehow I managed to hit that final note, but I then nearly lost my voice for the rest of the evening and kept coughing and gasping into a glass of water that Chris had to keep refilling. I also had to make several stops on the way home, so, when Chris suggested that we kept the song in for future appearances, I wasn't that keen

at first. In the end, I had to agree as it had gone down very
well and the audiences loved it, but, when I do it these days,
I need the assistance of some very tight underwear to help
me reach that cruel final C!

One of the nicest things about this work is that it gives me
an overview of how the Church is faring in the UK. I know
that the media and others seem to think that the Church
is dying, but my experience has been quite the opposite.
Perhaps some of the smaller country parishes *are* suffering
from a dying local population and the younger people are
not replacing them, but most of the churches I have been to
have been bubbling with life. Since that first night, I have
been up to Scotland, across to Wales, the West Country and
even the Isle of Man. Wherever I go, the churches are plainly
alive and well. It doesn't seem to matter what denomination
they are either. From Methodist to Anglican and Free Church
to Baptist, the churches are often large, strong and playing
a vital part in the lives of their local communities. We are
living in dangerous times and there is a lot of anxiety about
the future. The message of the gospel brings hope, encouragement and security at a time when it has never been more
needed.

A few years after that first gig for 1500 people, I would
never have dreamt that I would be standing in front of 4000
at a Louis Palau event. I was gobsmacked when this amazing
speaker came on and spent an hour talking about all my own
experiences and linking them to his preaching. It was as if
God had melded the two parts together. As I listened, I was
deeply moved to see my own life reflected back to me and
how much God had come to my rescue.

When I do my gospel gigs now, I say what I truly believe,
which is that I would never have got through all my personal
traumas in one piece had it not been for God's help, support
and guidance. Most recently, I have finished my spot with a
song called 'Footsteps', recorded by Daniel O'Donnell. It's a

musical version of the famous prayer in which a traveller questions the Lord about the fact that when he needed God the most, there was only one set of footprints in the sand. God explains that when the traveller was going through the most difficult time, God was actually carrying him and the one set of footprints is God's. It's a wonderfully succinct way of putting exactly what had happened to me, so it's a great way to finish.

The most dramatic appearance was at an open-air event in the middle of a town square in Dorset. I was on stage talking about Paul, when this man started to shout out at me.

'You don't know what you're talking about!' he screamed.

I looked across at Chris, who was interviewing me, and his eyes suggested that we just carry on. The man's shouting got louder and louder, though, so it was very difficult to continue. The audience was becoming very uneasy and those nearest him began to try to move away. Just when I thought we couldn't carry on, three big burly policemen appeared and tried to grab him. The man was having none of this and a huge struggle ensued, with the man being pinned down on the floor and put in handcuffs.

We carried on to the end and later I learned that the man was well known to the police. He had recently had his children taken away from him. I felt very sorry for him and, in a peculiar sort of way, knew something of what he was going through.

A Scottish gospel tour we did in 2000 became a turning point in my life. We spent four days playing to audiences across the highlands and lowlands among the most beautiful scenery imaginable. The venues were just as varied. One was a 1970s church built in the middle of a very tough Motherwell housing estate. It was so rough that the church was actually surrounded by barbed wire! Inside, there was the most modern, state-of-the-art equipment I had ever seen. I had to keep stopping to look at myself being projected on to a huge video screen behind me.

In contrast to this, at a church in Falkirk, the lights fused in the middle of the show and we had to continue with just one overhead bulb. Otherwise, though, there was one similarity – the church secretary locked our cars up in a compound while we were on stage!

After the show that night, a woman came up to me to say that her son was also a heroin addict and was going through all the things that I had mentioned about Paul during the evening. She asked if I would pray for her and it was the first time I had ever done anything like this, so I was pretty shaky. She seemed happy with the chat and prayer, though, and said that she had felt stronger and more able to deal with the problems that faced her and her son.

Falkirk was followed by Glasgow, where a huge inner-city church that had been abandoned had been purchased by another fellowship that was outgrowing its own buildings. Consequently, a newish church was reviving an old one.

Before that, Chris and I were special guests at a Sunday morning service in another church where there was a very powerful preacher. He'd come all the way from London to be there, so Chris felt quite at home.

When we arrived for the evening gig, we found ourselves outside a church that looked quite derelict. It took us ten minutes to find a door that was open and, when we went inside, it smelt of damp and mothballs.

'Oh dear,' we said to each other. 'This is going to be a hard place to work in.'

We were there to provide an evening of fun and faith to set the ball rolling for the restoration of this old building, but the atmosphere there seemed to make this possibility a little daunting. The church was very large, almost like a cathedral, and the echo made me feel like I was in a cave.

I needn't have worried. When 7.30 p.m. came, the place

was packed with young and old alike. The church had gone from deathly quiet to buzzing and it reminded me of the difference an audience can make.

The pews were due to be replaced with new seating, but were obviously hard on people's bottoms that night. I didn't know, but they were originally made like this to try to prevent the congregation from falling asleep during sermons!

Once again it was very strange singing my Buddy Holly medley in such a venue, but everyone clapped and cheered along, so all was well. Halfway through our chat, Chris completely confused me by asking everybody to stand up and stretch their legs. I thought he'd got fed up with our chat and was going to ask everybody to leave!

There couldn't have been a greater contrast between this church and our final venue. After a lovely drive through Kinross, we passed the famous Gleneagles Hotel, but, as I'm a useless golfer, I wasn't tempted to drop in.

'Good job I haven't got Eddie with me,' I thought.

The church was near Perth and at first seemed to be someone's home, with a shop at the front. This wasn't far short of the truth, though, and I now always call it the upper room gig.

Climbing the rambling but newly decorated stairs into a lovely bright room with a tiny stage, the previous night's cavern suddenly seemed a million miles away.

'How many people are coming tonight?' I asked the organizer.

'We don't know yet,' he replied. 'We've given away some free tickets, so we don't really know until people turn up.'

A quick calculation of the seats in the room made it just over 100 and we seemed to be a bit out in the country so about 50 or so people would come, I guessed.

After the sound check, Chris and I relaxed in a little room next to the main room as we waited to see who would arrive.

There was a knock at the door.

'Sorry chaps, but could we borrow your seats?'

'Sure,' I said. 'But what's the problem?'

'We've run out of chairs and yours are the only two left!'

When Chris introduced me and I walked out on stage, I couldn't believe my eyes. The place was absolutely crammed to capacity. There were people sitting on the counter at the side where they served tea, bodies crouched on the floor all along the sides, people standing at the back and a whole row of people sitting at my feet on the stage, as if they were footlights, with their heads craned so that they could see me. I made some crack about it being like the upper room in the story of the last supper. We had a wonderful evening.

The whole tour was like a breath of fresh air. After all the difficulties I had been going through with the family, it felt like I had been given a short, but boosting holiday. I have also found that when I'm on what I now call 'God's business', somehow other things in my life are sorted out along the way.

For most of my life with Little and Large, there had always been someone else to take care of things – a manager to guide our career, an agent to provide and keep a diary of the bookings, an accountant to take care of everything financial, a roadie to transport our gear, a stage manager to arrange the theatre facilities and even dressers to help us with our costumes.

There was also a feeling floating around inside me of having been at the mercy of others. Throughout our career, while it was nice to have other people make the decisions, it sometimes felt as if my life was not my own. I never felt that I could say to my agent, 'No, I can't do that gig in May because it's my son's birthday.' Work still came first in everything and, although that is the nature of the showbiz world, in all honesty I was getting a bit fed up with being like a puppet.

During the Scottish tour, God started to talk to me about becoming more independent. I don't mean that I was hearing voices in my head, but little things that were said by various people I met on the tour and by Chris seemed to connect all at once somehow. I had a bit of a pray about it, too, and went home determined to see what I could do to be more in control of my own life.

Apart from the Scottish venues, I've played gospel gigs in some unusual places, too. Woodville Prison was one! This establishment is multifunctional, catering for high-security prisoners, including suspected terrorists, life sentence prisoners and others who are facing serious criminal charges. In addition, there are young offenders, prisoners charged with serious sexual offences and those who have been identified as some of the most difficult, dangerous and violent in the prison system.

When Dave Berry, a trustee of Christians in Entertainment, and Chris asked me about the possibility of appearing there, they didn't give me all these details! If they had, perhaps I would have thought twice about going. As it was, I was persuaded to perform an abridged version of my gospel show one Sunday afternoon, sandwiched between gigs I was doing the previous evening and later that night.

Dave, a senior probation officer, had been sent the request for me to appear by the prison chaplain and I'm glad Dave suggested that he drove us to the prison and attend with us because it was a pretty frightening experience.

Having been to secure institutions because of Paul, I thought that I would be prepared for anything, but I was wrong. As we approached the very new-looking building sprawled over quite a wide area near Milton Keynes, I saw the huge wire fence and something inside me sank. I was thrilled to be able to offer a little hope and encouragement to those inside, but I knew that they were unlikely to be my normal type of audience.

This was confirmed when I nonchalantly asked Dave what sort of inmates the prison contained. He was halfway through

telling me when I noticed a different sort of television camera
to the one I was used to scanning all the occupants of our
car. The gate eventually opened and we were ushered into a
parking space for visitors.

Now on foot, we started the long process of making our
way towards the venue where I was to perform. From the
reception office, it felt like there were 20 different locks and
doors that we went through. As each door slammed behind
me, I wondered how I was ever going to get out.

We were searched several times – even Dave, who, as a
member of the prison authorities, I would have expected to
be exempt. My guitar and case were carefully inspected to
see if there was anything unusual. I held my breath and imagined what awful things might happen to me if, by some
strange quirk, they found an old penknife or something else
equally suspicious inside, like the last time with my friends!

After all the searching and unlocking and locking were
over, we were led to the governor's office. A warm and
friendly lady, she seemed to be completely out of keeping
with the rest of the environment that had greeted us.

'Welcome to Woodhill,' she said with a huge smile. 'We
just need to go through a few security measures.'

A very large prison officer took over and I started to crack
some joke about having thought I'd left Eddie behind. Noticing, however, that this huge man probably wasn't the type
to laugh much, I quickly decided against it.

'We have an unusual gathering of men from all departments
here today,' he began. 'We don't normally have any problems,
but this is a special occasion for us and you never know.'

My knees started to knock and I looked across at Dave
for some reassurance, but he looked as worried as I felt. Chris
was no help either. His face just stayed in a sort of fixed
smile and I considered that perhaps someone had removed
his batteries, leaving this expression frozen on his screen.

'If there is any problem with the men at all, we request

that you move as quickly as possible to a point in the room that we shall show you later,' he continued. 'It is here that you can be protected by my men and eventually led to safety.'

Now this really didn't sound like Sunday night at the London Palladium!

After tea and cakes with the governor and some of her senior staff, we were led through another set of doors into the main hall – a sort of chapel come meeting place. The chaplain had set out the chairs in a semicircular plan, but it didn't feel like an amphitheatre at all.

We were just able to squeeze in a quick rehearsal and a sound balance check for my mic and guitar before the doors swung open and in walked a silent troop of men, the prisoners, and they looked very scary. I was going to perform in front of murderers and so on and when they were already looking at me it was very unnerving. All ages, every type of face, every sort of build, slowly made their way along the lines of chairs until every one was filled. There wasn't a single smile and almost complete silence – it was the most bizarre atmosphere.

The prison chaplain was a complete contrast to all this and he was extremely excited.

'Welcome to our special event,' he said loudly in the most eager way. 'We have from stage and television one half of comedy duo Little and Large and I know you are going to have a fantastic time.'

Looking across at the faces in front of me, I wasn't so sure he was telling the truth.

Now it was Chris' turn to warm them up a little and introduce me as he always does. At least none of them could walk out, I pondered, or ask for their money back!

I saw Dave standing at the back, nervously shifting from one foot to another, obviously anxious that all would go well. He threw an encouraging smile my way as Chris introduced me and I bounced on to the platform.

'Hello, my name's Syd Little and I expect you know what yours is!' was how I started. Without allowing any pause, I went straight into Buddy Holly and was simply astounded when they started to clap and sing along. By the time I had finished the eight-minute medley of his greatest hits, they were laughing and smiling right on cue.

The rest of the hour went very well and most of them were quite receptive. It was clear to see that some really related to my story of Paul, the nodding heads and agreeing grunts I found very moving. I think they associated themselves with many of the difficulties that I had experienced in my life. It seemed that they were becoming less like prisoners and more like unfortunate people in tough situations. If things hadn't gone the way they had for me, perhaps I would be in here, too, I thought as I sang another song.

As we were specifically asked by the chaplain to finish with a question and answer sessions, Chris created the opportunity and a number of hands shot up.

The first question was asked by a very intelligent-looking man in his late forties with some sort of paperwork in his hand. It threw me completely. I was expecting something about God or showbusiness, but, instead, it was about a new EU agreement that, had it not been brought in, he would not be in prison now and what did I think of that?

Chris fielded it very well, because I didn't even understand the question, let alone have an answer, so I just said that I was a comedian, not a politician. In a last-minute panic, I looked at him and thought that I might have upset him. So, in an effort to avoid being placed on his target list, I quickly added that I hoped he would find the answer to his quandary soon!

A few more relevant questions followed and, before long, it was time to finish. When the chaplain said a final prayer and thanked everyone for coming, I expected the gathering of men to flow back out through the door they had used when they arrived, but the opposite happened and several of the men rushed towards me in a most menacing fashion. Half expecting him to pull out a knife, one man thrust forward an empty hand. So it was that I found myself shaking hands with some of the most notorious prisoners in the country.

The visit really opened my eyes to what being in prison is really all about. As I met a very relieved-looking Dave, I said that I could never cope with being in prison and it was certainly very different from the image that some have of it as being just a glorified holiday camp.

On the way out, the chaplain presented us with a mug. It had 'Property of HM Prison Woodhill' printed on it and I'm very proud to own it.

Another interesting gig was in an Indian restaurant! The church had hired the venue for the evening and invited lots of people, so the place was packed and there wasn't a lot of room to stand and sing to the sound of poppadums being eaten. I did manage it, even though I was at the back of the restaurant facing the window at the front and passers by were peering in wondering why I was there. One man walked back and forth past the window so many times that it completely threw me, I forgot the words of the song and had to start all over again. Twice!

I think that the evening was God having a bit of a laugh because I'm a sucker for curry. If I'm away from home for a season or on tour, I have to try to ration myself as I could easily enjoy one every night. I can eat quite hot ones – I've even managed a vindaloo. I'm happier with a jalfrezi, though, and even mentioning it now is making my taste buds tingle.

Showbusiness is a funny, topsy-turvy world because I go to work when everyone else is coming home and sometimes go to bed when everyone else is getting up. After work, most people go home and relax rather than go straight to bed and, despite my hours, I'm the same. When I finish work, even if it's 1 a.m., I can't just hop into bed. As most restaurants and pubs are closed by this time, the choice is either Indian or Chinese.

My passion for curry started back in the late 1960s when the curry houses were just being opened in the UK. The first one I went to was in Jackson Street, Moss Side, Manchester. It was quite normal then to have a bowl of curry with chips and bread and butter. It was in this northern restaurant, which was a bit spit and sawdust, that three men were trying to leave without paying the bill. I saw the manager throw curry powder in the eyes of one of them and he ran off shrieking. I bet he made sure to always pay his bill after that!

It all became a bit more sophisticated in the 1970s when they started serving rice, Bombay duck and onion bhaji – all of which I have been hooked on for the years. A favourite haunt was the Taj Mahal in Ealing where it seemed that the whole of the showbiz world would hang out. One day, Sheree and I popped in there for a quick meal and saw Cliff Richard sitting at the opposite table. I couldn't resist going over, saying hello and thanking him for the new record he had just released in our honour, 'A Little in Love'. I'm glad he got the joke. We had been appearing with Cliff at the Palladium, so I found out that Cliff is partial to a curry too, even at 2 a.m.!

After every TV show, we would go around the corner to an Indian restaurant in Shepherd's Bush and start to analyze the show. We would sit there with the producers and directors, discussing which bits we thought worked and which ones didn't and, for me, the Indian meal afterwards was even better than recording the actual show.

Sitting there one day, we came up with the idea of doing a sketch in an Indian restaurant and, rather than bother the BBC props department, we ordered all the food fresh from the manager, who was very pleased. I'm surprised that we didn't get severely told off, though, because, when we brought all the dishes in, we seemed to fill BBC television centre with the aroma of chicken tikka masala. People were walking down the corridors looking around, salivating and wondering where the aroma was coming from.

We put a huge pile of poppadums on a table and dressed Eddie as a t'ai chi expert who was supposed to chop them all in half before delivering them to a customer. It worked fine in rehearsal, with a loud crunch and bits shooting off in all directions. When he tried to chop them for the actual recording, however, it was a different story. The pile just melted away beneath his hand like a pack of cards because we hadn't remembered that poppadums soak up moisture from the air and become soft. We had to send one of the crew back round to the restaurant to order another huge pile. The manager must have thought it was his lucky day. Of course, the best bit about all this was eating the food after-wards. Apart from the poppadums that is!

You have to be careful of course. Some curries don't always agree with you, as I found on stage one night while singing a song called 'Mule Skinner Blues'. The song has a very long last note – 16 bars long, in fact. I got halfway through this final burst when I felt something happen 'downstairs' and had to rush off the stage. I left Eddie there wondering what was happening. He turned to the audience and said, 'It must have been the curry he had last night!' and in this case it was true.

At the Casino Club in Bolton, the problem was at the other end. It was a cabaret venue and Eddie saw me getting whiter and whiter until I eventually ran off stage to be violently sick on the floor in the wings. I then took a tissue from the stage hand and went straight back on stage, only to find that the entire audience had now stopped eating their dinner. They must have heard the whole thing and it had seriously affected their appetites! It didn't help that Eddie made a running gag out of it that lasted throughout the rest of our performance.

I bet the meal takings that night were the lowest they had seen for a long time.

I've never been ill for a gospel gig, but I did look very unwell on a poster one day. I arrived at the town and, as I whizzed past all the shops in the High Street, I noticed a lot of publicity for a black man doing a special evening in a local church. With one eye on the road and the other on the posters, I noticed that his name was also Syd Little. What a coincidence, I thought! When I stopped the car and started to unload my gear into the venue, I saw that the poster had been so badly photocopied that all you could see was a black face with white teeth and white glasses. I wondered if the audience would be surprised when they saw me that night, so we had lots of fun talking about this all the way through the show.

These gigs, over a five-year period, changed my life in many ways. One of the most important was learning that, even after being part of a double act for so long, the performance gifts that had originally enabled me to entertain as a solo act were still there. As audiences laughed, shouted, cheered and clapped, my confidence was boosted and now the act that I do in my gospel set works really well. So well, in fact, that I would love to go back to that first date in Eaglescliffe and do it properly for them this time!

I have been criticized for making a charge for my appearances, though this is a fraction of what I would be paid normally. There are several reasons for this. I have to cover my time and expenses, and Chris' too. Despite what people may think, I am not a millionaire! It also covers the cost of the publicity we produce and the wonderful back-up that Nick Page gives at Shorehill Arts. We still have a lot of people call who have never attempted a church evening like this and Nick is very thorough and patient in guiding them on how to enjoy a successful evening.

To some very strict Christians who might say, 'Don't you

think that the gospel should be given without charge?' I reply, 'Don't you pay your minister then?'

On an earlier try-out gospel show, there was an evening where a wannabe entrepreneur decided that he would use the event to make himself rich. Tickets were sold at a huge price and so hardly anyone turned up. The evening was a complete disaster because money isn't the reason for the event, just the vehicle to help it happen.

In the early days when we did some gigs for nothing, we found that the organizers didn't get behind it 100 per cent. There's a little verse in the Bible that says something like 'Where your treasure is, there is also your heart'. This I have found to be totally true. When money is involved, people start to take it seriously. The preparation is more thorough and the event is taken to heart.

Money brings value, too. Generally, if you give a free ticket for an event to a stranger in the street, it doesn't have as much value or importance attached to it as one for which they would have needed to pay. They can take it or leave it because there's no commitment.

Also, if it's free, they will immediately wonder what the catch is. They might think that I'm about to sell them a time-share or something. Even worse, I might actually preach at them! In our society, we are used to paying for something that we want. Churches that ask a small price for a ticket seem to be among the most successful.

I know that some organizers use our evening as part of an ongoing string of free community events and that's fine, but, generally, if someone pays to go to the theatre or cinema, it means that they have expectations of what they will get in return. There's nothing I like better than to work in front of an expectant audience – and I don't mean a room full of pregnant women, though someone did go into labour during one of my songs once.

Some of my professional colleagues scoffed at the idea of

doing gospel gigs, but when one or two came to see me and there was a packed-out, buzzing audience, they were amazed and some asked me if they could do shows like it themselves! Some suggested that church audiences were easy.

'They're on your side before you even begin,' one comic told me. 'You're just preaching to the converted.'

Well, for one thing, I don't preach and I have actually found the opposite of what he suggested to be true. For a start, most of the venues are church-based, so people are not automatically in the mood to be entertained, which they would be if they were in a theatre. Also, a great many people come who are not used to going to church. They've come because they are intrigued as to why Syd Little should be appearing in their town in such an unusual place. Thus, my audiences never know what to expect. They don't know if I'm going to preach or tap dance, so they are often a little nervous and need to be put at their ease. There are lots of barriers to be overcome before I can get the audience to relax, but, as I tell the hilarious story of Little and Large and then my own personal story, laughter and tears soon mix.

People still come to see me with, 'Well we know what Eddie does, but what does Syd do?' written on their faces, but at least if you've read this you'll know!

I remember that I did a charity spot for the Salvation Army with Bobby Ball. Bobby was keen to make me feel relaxed because I was quite new to the game and the audience was full of drug addicts. I had been asked to come to chat about my experiences with Paul.

'You'll be preaching next!' said Bobby as I sat and waited for my introduction.

'Never,' said I.

We both did our bits and, when we came off, Bobby said:

'I thought you said that you would never preach? That's just what you have done!'

He was right. I know some people think of a sermon as a

good excuse to slide down in the pew and have a quick sleep. Good preaching, though, is full of life, vitality and hope.

My gospel show is certainly entertaining, but it is challenging, too, and Chris continues to throw in new questions each time, just to keep me on my toes. At a recent gospel gig near Bracknell, I was on the stage talking about the usual things when a sudden thought popped into my head. God doesn't always talk to me in such a direct way, but this I knew was straight from heaven.

'There may be some people here today who, like me, have been going through some tough times,' I started. 'But I have to say that where there is a winter, a spring is sure to follow.'

The words were so profound, they didn't seem to come from me. I looked around for a moment, almost as if I was expecting someone else to have spoken them or that I was perhaps just reading the words of a hymn. Afterwards, I was inundated with people coming up and saying that those words were just for them. What I said had given them hope and encouraged them to not give up but hang on and see their situation through. I was thrilled because it meant that my own difficulties were now helping others.

Little did I know that, in all of this, God was actually preparing me for something else. He had a secondary plan that was about to be launched in my life and I couldn't see it at this moment in time. In the months to come, my professional life was to change so much and this fresh experience of working solo was to become a lifesaver.

9

AN UNEXPECTED TURN

In my case, the Paradise Room didn't live up to the expectations that its name had created in my mind. It was a great cabaret venue to work in and was a new venture, specially built for the Thompson family who own and run Blackpool's famous pleasure beach. Plush tables, 800 comfortable seats arranged in a horseshoe, a late-running bar and plenty of families made it a very lively place from early evening until cabaret time at 9 p.m., which was when we were on.

We did one show a night for the long season that ran from June to November, which coincided with the illuminations. I always thought the luxurious room contrasted greatly with the backstage facilities, which were very basic. We even had to walk through the kitchens to get to our dressing rooms, which was a bit embarrassing if we ever had backstage visitors. If I hadn't eaten that day, the aroma of barbecued chicken would make my mouth water the whole evening. I understand that Frank Sinatra had the same kinds of facilities in Las Vegas, so we were in good company!

The Paradise Room was cleverly marketed because if a family bought a certain number of tickets for the pleasure beach rides, they got free tickets for the Paradise Room that evening. This meant that the room was full every night throughout the season and the bar and food takings made up for any reduction in income that resulted from giving out the free tickets. For us, the only problem was that the combination of younger children and a lot of music early on meant that the younger families were often in a very fidgety and tired state by the time we came on. So, we just shouted louder to be heard over all the extra activity!

The Paradise Room has one very special memory for me – the first time Donna came out since she was attacked, she came here. Indeed, she stayed with us for the summer. She had regained full use of her hands and was well on the mend. Coming out with us for the first time was such an encouraging sign and I was so excited that things were moving forward.

Peering through the curtains at the side of the stage, I could see her sitting on the red velvet seat, surrounded by friends and family, all laughing and giggling away. As I watched in secret, a tear fell from one eye on to my shiny patent leather shoe and I wondered if I would be able to keep my composure while performing in front of her.

'Ladies and gentlemen, you will please welcome the stars of the evening . . . here they are . . . Little and Large!'

As the orchestra struck up our opening music, we launched into:

> Everybody, needs somebody
> Everybody, needs somebody,
> I need you, you, you.
> I need you, you, you . . .

I was soon choking back the tears before we'd even started our comedy routine.

The spot we did that night was one of the most enjoyable and fulfilling of my life. It felt like all the spring days full of sunshine and flowers had arrived at once. Towards the end, Eddie unexpectedly stepped forward away from me, but with a serious look on his face and I could see something surprising was coming.

'Ladies and gentlemen,' said Eddie, 'I just want to thank

you for being a wonderful audience, but none more wonderful than one particular lady here tonight. I'm sure you've read about her in the papers, but Syd's daughter is here and she's looking as well as ever. Please give a big round of applause for Donna!'

With that, the spotlight fell on Donna and she stood up to rapturous applause from the entire audience.

I mouthed a 'Thank you' to Eddie. I was so proud, but by this time, my eyes were overflowing and, even though the applause was still ringing in my ears, I couldn't get off the stage quickly enough. Now, every time I think or talk about that evening, I still shed a tear or two.

As Donna was improving, Eddie's heart was getting weaker and weaker. Seeing him arrive at the theatre each day looking greyer and greyer, I began to fear the worst. Eddie was already suffering from gout and this was affecting his balance more and more. He always gave 100 per cent once on stage, but there were times when he was in so much pain that I winced to see how much he was struggling. He sometimes found it difficult to stand up and, once on his feet, it was difficult to move. His knees were suffering because of his weight and now his heart was starting to buckle under the strain as well. Something had to be done, I thought.

On stage, it meant that I was always on tenterhooks, wondering if we would actually get through the whole hour-long routine without him collapsing. I couldn't relax and I knew that it must be affecting our performance. It was all very stressful and one particularly bad night, when I could see that Eddie was in agony, it all suddenly felt like a dream as I stood on stage and looked down at all these people laughing. 'If only they knew,' I thought. 'They wouldn't be laughing then.'

In an effort to compensate each night, I would try to increase how energetic I was being on stage, but all the pacing up and down only meant that the act started to look very uneven and I could feel that things were not right between us on stage any more. The laughs still came thick and fast, but I think this was more down to our experience and Eddie's skill, than creativity. Eddie's condition caused constant breathlessness, but he always found enough energy to avoid letting his audience down. That was until November 1996 – the last night of our season at the Paradise Room.

I arrived at the theatre only to see lots of activity around the dressing rooms and I instantly knew something was amiss.

'Eddie's off sick,' said Derek, our roadie. 'He can't make it tonight.'

As I sat in the empty dressing room, I heard the theatre manager's voice ring out over the intercom: 'Ladies and gentlemen. I'm sorry to announce that Little and Large will not be appearing tonight.' It was as simple and clinical as that and I felt terrible that we had let so many people down on what was for them a special night out.

'I must go on stage and apologize,' I told the manager.

As I stepped out on stage without my partner for the first time in 30 years, it was a most bizarre feeling.

'I'm sorry that we can't perform for you tonight,' I said to the silent crowd. 'But at least we shall be back next year!' I blurted, because we had already been invited back in 1997.

It wasn't the most sensitive thing to say. Loose Lips Little hadn't twigged that explaining we would be back at a later date wasn't going to help the 400 people who had booked to see Little and Large *that* night! Thank goodness for super-sub Frank Carson, who went on in our place and 'stormed 'em'.

After a few weeks recovering, we were back on the road for a few one-nighters before launching into panto at the Cliffs Pavilion, Southend-on-Sea. Panto would prove to be the worst thing for Eddie's health as it is so demanding, but by now it was our main source of income. We were booked to do anything from 12 to 15 shows each week, so everyone in the cast had to make sure that they had the energy to cope.

Some days we were to do three shows. One at 10 a.m., one at 2.30 p.m. and another at 7.30 p.m. The first day this happened, by the time I got to the 7.30 p.m. performance, I couldn't remember whether it was the last half of the first show or the first half of the last show or what? Thank goodness for my dresser, who just shunted me from one place to another and plonked the appropriate costume on me, which gave me some clue as to what I was supposed to be doing.

On New Year's Day, I rushed on stage dressed as a Chinese policeman once more, only to discover Eddie looking very grey. As we went through our scene together, my eyes met his and we began talking a different, silent language to the one that was making the audience laugh. By some miracle, he made it through to the end of the show and then collapsed in a heap in his dressing room. The management sent him home and he drove straight back to Bristol. It was suspected that he had suffered a stroke. We knew that he had problems with his heart.

Just by seeing how ill he looked, it was clear that he would not be able to work for some while and I prepared myself for making our double act into a solo performance once more – quite difficult if you are a Chinese policeman! Fortunately, my long experience and the confidence-building effect of my solo gospel gigs now supported me as I faced the audience alone. I can't say that I didn't panic at all, but I worked through the script with the other members of the cast, including Jonathan Morris, who was playing Aladdin.

With Eddie, I always knew that I was overly generous in letting him have all the punchlines, even though I was supposed to be the stooge. So, when we sat down in Jonathan's dressing room to decide who would get Eddie's lines in the panto, I automatically assumed he would want them.

'No, Syd,' said Jonathan. 'You have that line. You take the laugh.'

'Are you sure?' said I.

'Absolutely,' said Jonathan.

I ended up doing the squeaky voice and plenty of extra gags and, I must admit, I relished the new material. I got plenty of new laughs, but I soon stopped laughing when I realized that the producers of the show were not going to book us for pantos in the future. We had worked with some of the biggest showbusiness organizations for over 30 years, so it felt like we had been naughty boys. If I had had a tail, it would have been firmly between my legs! The fact is that showbusiness is often cruel. When you are making people a lot of money, the red carpet is put out for you. When things change, many of those who have been around you for a long time seem to disappear.

Only one lady had wanted a refund for her ticket for the panto when she heard that Eddie was not appearing, but the management cut our salary in half, despite the fact that the box office earnings remained the same.

People in the business were noticing how ill Eddie looked and gossip is rife in our world. The word was that Little and Large were becoming an unreliable act, which wasn't true, but everything is exaggerated by the Chinese whispers effect. We were faced with a serious problem. With no television work and summer seasons having all but dried up, becoming one-nighters instead, panto was still the best earner for the year. How would we manage without it? I carried on until the end of what turned out to be a very successful run, but I feared that this could be our last Christmas season together.

Eddie was back home by now and visiting the hospital for all kinds of tests. There was some talk of a major heart problem that could only be rectified by surgery.

Not one to sit around and mope, I thought about how I would fill in my time while Eddie recovered and made some decisions about the future. There were several gospel gigs in my diary and I was looking forward to those, but I needed something else to fill my time.

On the performance front, I had a call from a local hotel in Blackpool, asking if I could step in for them one night as their cabaret performer was off sick. I jumped at the chance and, dusting off my amps and guitar in the shed, decided that I would play the music that I enjoyed – something that I had not done for years.

'It's wonderful to be able to appear before you tonight, ladies and gentlemen,' I announced when I got to the gig and stepped onto the tiny stage. 'I'm afraid Eddie isn't here tonight, but at least it means that I can sing a song all the way through without him butting in!'

This was not only a true statement, but one that helped to start the evening off with a big laugh. At the end of my 40-minute spot, they were still cheering me on, so I stayed another hour and a half singing every song I knew!

'Well, ladies and gentlemen,' said the manager afterwards. 'Most acts that come here do 20 minutes and they're off. You certainly get your money's worth with Syd Little!'

After all that singing, I was pretty hoarse by the time I got home, so Sheree had a very quiet couple of days while my voice recovered.

Alongside this local cabaret work, I decided to use some of my time to do some decorating for some friends and family. I never lost my painting and wallpapering skills and often find it really therapeutic and relaxing. I even offered to help out Dominic's school by decorating its observatory. Not many schools have one of those. It sits in the middle of the rugby field and has been there since the nineteenth century. It was originally built by the holiday firm Thompson – something that it was famous for in the 1800s. As far as we know, there are only two of these in the world. One is in New Zealand and the other is here in Fleetwood.

For many years, the lovely telescope had stood in the observatory, which was open to vandals. One day they went in and tried to burn it down. They didn't succeed, but it was

I've just discovered Sheree is pregnant with our 'miracle baby'. 1988.

Michael Aspel surprises us on-stage in 1993 for 'This is your Life'.

They're behind you! With Frank Bruno in Panto.

Dominic and Sheree. What a
handsome family!

Entertaining the troops in the Falklands. 1996. Still the fashion leader.

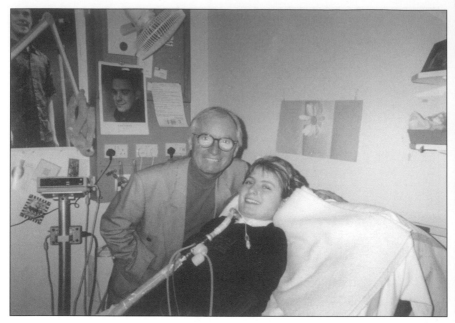

Visiting brave Hannah in Alder Hey Hospital with Robbie looking on.

With my all-time comedy hero and friend Norman Collier.

Going solo and supporting the marvellous Joe Longthorne. Blackpool North Pier 2003.

Just waiting for an audience. Rehearsing 'An Evening with Syd Little', with Chris Gidney 2004.

With Darren Day.
Sunderland Empire 2004.

My first solo Panto with Darren Day
and Jean Fergusson.

My Fairy Godmother, Jean Fergusson.

Sheree and I with the vicar from *Dad's Army* Frank Williams, and an up and coming pop star!

'Rock Around the Church' with Cannon and Ball, Diane Regan and Chris. I was told I was having my picture taken by David Bailey but it was David Bayley! Thanks David!

My trusty leaning post!

left derelict until a new astronomy teacher joined the school and drummed up a campaign to have it restored. I volunteered and there were looks of surprise on many faces. The money and labour were gathered to begin work and I went out and bought some new brushes. Over the next few weeks, the dilapidated building was transformed into a bright, inviting new arena in which to discover the universe and the old telescope was brought back to its glistening state once more.

On the night of the big unveiling, all those involved in its refurbishment were invited to a very special late-night party. As I was given a large glass of red wine, a strange rumbling noise signalled that the roof was being winched open to reveal a huge crescent moon. As one of my favourite movies is *First Men in the Moon*, I was particularly excited! Suddenly, all the lights were turned off and, as if on cue, all the stars began to glisten and twinkle down on us through the open roof. We all took it in turns to look into the eyepiece of the solid brass telescope and I couldn't wait until I could take a look. I was like a kid at the seaside waiting impatiently for the other person's money to run out on one of those promenade telescopes so that I could jump in and have a go.

'Your turn, Syd!' said a very proud Nick Lister, the astronomy teacher. He's definitely the next Patrick Moore, you know.

'Thanks for your help in getting this up and running, Syd. Do you know that it is now connected to a computer so we can send pictures of what you see here anywhere at all? The hut in the middle of a field that no one took any notice of is now known throughout the world.'

'It's amazing!' was all I could think of to say.

Soon I was gazing through a tiny hole and up and out into the vast expanse of the heavens. My immediate reaction was to feel very small.

'How can they say that this galaxy is all some mistake?' I mumbled to myself. To me, the practical proof of God's existence was now literally staring me in the face. I looked intently at the three-quarter moon. I could see the craters. I squinted and said:

'The Moon looks lovely, but I can't see Neil Armstrong's footprints!'

Everyone laughed, but I don't think it helped subdue the patience of the next person waiting to use the giant telescope.

As I stood aside, lots of thoughts filled my mind. We still don't know what is in the heavens – only God knows – but scanning across all the bright stars in their multitudes made me think of how much fun God must have had putting it all together. Why has he created only one? Perhaps he has created other worlds, too, and maybe we shall see them one day?

'Isn't it good that God gives us knowledge a bit at a time?' I said to Sheree standing beside me. 'If we had it all at one time, humankind just couldn't take it all in. From the Stone Age, to the Iron Age, the Industrial Age and now the Nuclear Age. It's all been a slow process.'

When I returned a few weeks later, I just had to have a quick peek. Yes, it was full of schoolchildren, all bubbling with excitement. This gave me a sense of great satisfaction. On the way out, I turned and saw a small plaque on the wall that said the observatory had been '. . . decorated by Mr Syd Little'. I blushed to myself a little and thought that this will probably be the only little blue plaque I ever get!

The observatory project seemed to open the doors for further requests for help and I was soon asked if I could do more work at the school. This time it was for the outside, which was in real need of scrubbing down and repainting. It was a warm and glorious spring, so I was quite keen to get to work and perhaps boost my tan at the same time.

Most of the school staff and pupils were quite bemused at seeing me in my overalls and shouted out all sorts of encouraging remarks as they went past. Every time the school bell rang and there was a change of class I'd get, 'Lovely shade of white, Syd!' or 'Keep up the good work, Syd!' shouted up my ladder.

I was halfway along one of the outside walls when I heard a click below me. I looked down and there were two men, one with a camera and one with a notebook. My professional instinct told me what this was all about, even before they opened their mouths.

'We hear you're now working as a painter and decorator, Syd. Is business that bad?'

After my many bad experiences with the press, my mouth shut like a clam and I refused to give an interview, but said that I was just helping out at the school. They asked me to look glum and I felt silly doing so because I was actually feeling very happy. I knew that the gloomy picture would be the one that they would use and rang Eddie for some advice.

'Well, whatever you do, they'll still print it,' he said.

He was right. The next day I hardly dared walk within a hundred yards of a newsagent, but there, on the front page of *The Star*, was the headline 'Matt Broke Syd Little!', showing the paintbrush in my hand. They had obviously taken a series of photos from different angles and, as I suspected, chosen the one that made me look the grumpiest. It was so awful I hardly recognized myself.

I found out later that someone in the school had supposedly called the newspaper and sold the story. I was angry more than anything, though worried that it may fuel some bullying for Dominic at school. The most hurtful thing was that it wasn't really true and, even if it was, surely it would have been better for me to earn some money doing a decent and honest day's work than to have gone on the dole.

I've got a great set of mates – John Kelley, David Swaine, Rob Nelder, Mark Steele, Paul King and many others – and, after seeing me in the papers, they decided that they would all give me jobs to do in their houses. This actually kept me going through the early lean times while I struggled to get my own identity as a solo act. The funniest thing was that, when they returned home and took a look at my work, they were pleasantly surprised.

'Wow, Syd. That's fantastic!' they would cry.

'Well, I was a professional painter and decorator from when I was 16 to 21, before I went into showbiz,' I reminded them.

'But we can't see the joins in the wallpaper!' they exclaimed.

'Oh, I think I could show Laurence Llewelyn-Bowen a thing or two,' I replied.

Although what the newspapers said caused Sheree and I some hurt, I refused to let something like this dictate how I lived my life. I would do what I felt was right, whatever people thought or said about me, so I continued to decorate my friends' and others' houses. One little old lady was very excited about me wallpapering her lounge, but kept expecting me to crack jokes as I slapped on the paste. She would make me a cup of tea and then stand there, looking longingly at me as if any minute I was sure to launch into the act. Another said: 'Hey, Syd, I'm going to put a little blue plaque outside my front door to say that our ceiling was painted by comedian Syd Little.' I thought it was a very funny idea, and would match the one inside the observatory. So, if you see anything like this on a front wall anywhere, you'll know it's for real.

One thing I discovered is that little old ladies will kill you with kindness. One would insist on cooking me a full three-course meal every lunchtime. Despite the fact that I had my own packed lunch, she insisted on feeding me to busting. We sat there chatting over the table for a long time and perhaps it was that I was helping to overcome her loneliness that made lunch more important than the decorating. Soup, ham salad and rice pudding meant that I could hardly work afterwards. It was a good thing she didn't offer me wine as well!

I still do some decorating today and love every opportunity I get. Also, I'm fitter than ever before and it's cheaper and easier than going to the gym. It's even better than knocking a little white ball around the green.

If I thought that the newspapers had already got their story, however, I was wrong. My friend Mark asked if I was busy and there was actually a break in my gigs schedule early in 2004, so, in the old thespian tradition I said I was 'resting'.

'I've got a factory that needs a lick of paint, Syd!'

I went and had a look and agreed to do it. It was a big job – too big really for one man and his ladder – but I was free, so I took it on. I was there for about three weeks and became a bit of a novelty with the factory workers: 'What's a millionaire like you doing this for, Syd?' was a constantly repeated question. I told them that I had read somewhere that one well-known British film star becomes a car mechanic between jobs simply because he loves doing it.

As I painted away, it reminded me of a true, now ironic, story about something that happened to me and Eddie when we were doing a season with Michael Barrymore as our guest in Eastbourne in 1982. A national newspaper wanted to do an article on what we were before we were famous. As Eddie was an electronics engineer, they fixed him up with plenty of plugs and cables, then handed me a brush and a paint pot. There we were, with me up the ladder pretending to paint and Eddie down below posing with a handful of wires as the photographer clicked away.

We must have looked an interesting sight because an old couple walked slowly past, staring us up and down. Then the old man suddenly shouted out in the most acrimonious manner, 'Thas never don a hard day's work in thar life!'

I was so irate to hear this because I had actually worked very hard, both before and during my time in showbusiness! It really upset me and I wanted to run after him and give him the true story. I did restrain myself, however, and so the cross look on my face in the *Daily Mail* on that occasion is perfectly genuine!

Normally Chris and I have an ongoing banter on and off the stage about southerners and northerners, with me saying us northerners are always the friendliest. However, on that occasion, it was certainly not true.

I was back working at Mark's factory in March 2004 when I heard a knock on the door. I was in the middle of munching my lunch and when I opened the door this voice said, 'Oh, it's true then. You are decorating. I'm from *The Sun* newspaper.'

He asked if he could take a picture and I said no.

'OK then,' he said and left.

I thought, aha, he's probably got one already. Apparently someone in the place where I was painting had snapped me on a mobile camera phone and then called the newspaper to try to sell the story once more.

I was flabbergasted that anyone would still be interested in a tale that had already been told years previously, but perhaps they were short on news items that week.

'Nice *Little* Earner', announced the headline, with a photo of me in my overalls again, squeezed in between a picture of Paris Hilton and an advert for Vauxhall cars. Apparently the article was even mentioned by Sarah Kennedy on her BBC Radio Two early morning show. I like Sarah so that's OK. I'm rather flattered in a way that people loved Little and Large so much that any gossip about us is still deemed newsworthy.

The interesting thing about this one was that, the same day, I got a call from the BBC saying that they were doing a pilot comedy show to be hosted by Gyles Brandreth. It was to be presented in the style of a home shopping channel, where they would give away items relating to each news story covered. I was asked if I would be interested in them filming me offering my services as a painter and decorator. I thought it was a very funny idea and agreed to take part.

Hat Trick productions is subcontracted by the BBC and responsible for popular series such as *Have I Got News For You*, so when the team arrived in Blackpool to film, I knew I was in safe hands.

'I'm Syd Little,' I said, standing outside a window with paint peeling off. 'I will come and decorate the room of your choice as long as it's no more than 15 feet square. I will undercoat and paint your ceilings, walls, windows, skirting boards and doors. Although I am literally not supersonic, I will be in and out in a day. If you are not completely satisfied, I will return with my steps back in amazement!' This was a corny line to finish with, but everybody seemed happy after a couple of takes and so off went the film crew back to London.

A few days later, I got a call from the production company.

'Syd, we're really sorry, but there's something wrong with the sound recording on the film we made of you. Would you mind if we came up to do it again?'

I didn't mind because I was paid again! If Ant and Dec or anyone else wants me to come and paint their studio, they can just give me a call.

There were some letters to the paper as a result of the article in the newspaper, including the following from a reader in Southampton:

'It was interesting to see comic Syd Little working as a painter and decorator. After [the newspaper] has shamed so many ordinary people too lazy to get a job, it was refreshing to see a famous entertainer happy to do a little manual labour.'

I'm not one to gloat, but I think I had the last laugh on this story. It all turned to my benefit in the end and reminded me how God is in the resurrection business. He's an expert at taking something negative and turning it around for good. This has certainly been true of the story of my life!

Just when we thought our days in panto were numbered, we were invited to the Beck Theatre in Hayes, Middlesex, to work for producer Charles Vance in 2000. It was a bit of a cold and damp season and all I seemed to do was eat, perform and sleep. I saw very little of Eddie outside the theatre and I was feeling a little lonely and sorry for myself, being far away from home – particularly as I had not been able to see my family for any length of time during the Christmas holidays. A six-hour-long midnight drive on Christmas Eve was followed by another six-hour-long snowcovered trek back down the following day.

When I arrived at the theatre, there was a message that someone had called and would pop back later. I didn't recognize the name, but when he called back and introduced himself as a local church minister, I remembered that Chris from CIE had mentioned that I may get a visit.

I invited him into my dressing room and we sat and chatted for some while about all sorts of things. His zest for life and passion for God lifted my spirits very quickly and a short prayer for friends and family left me feeling warm and happy inside. I got through the next few weeks of the panto with a new sprint in my step. I often think that it isn't so much the fact that God loves to encourage us that is his secret, but that his timing is perfect. When Chris visited me a few days later, he mentioned the Bible verse that says God has '. . . a hope and a future' for all of us and that includes me.

In the months that followed, I reminded myself of this. God did have some sort of a future for me, I believed, although, in the bleakness of a slowly dying career, it was difficult to visualize.

Also in the year 2000, Sheree and I celebrated our silver wedding anniversary. Not many showbiz marriages last that long, so we were very proud. We invited a host of family and friends to join us at Farmer Parr's Animal World. It's still a great fun place for anyone coming to Blackpool to visit and it's got plenty of funny characters – mainly two-legged ones! We sat on bales of hay, enjoying the hot sunny evening, ate some wonderful food, then went into the barn and enjoyed music from a live band, letting the champagne flow until very late.

Farmer Parr, James and his wife Deborah have become good friends and I have found that friends like these are so precious and so important. We would often sit and chat until the cows literally came home about anything and everything. Actually in the case of Farmer Parr it's llamas rather than cows.

That summer was a bit stop and start workwise. Eddie and our management were reluctant to take too many jobs on. We chose to do enough to keep us going, but not too much to exhaust Eddie, who insisted that he continue. Despite this, we drove over 30,000 miles around the UK that summer as we played in most of Warner's and Haven holiday camps. The money was good, the audiences were great, but Eddie's mood was terrible. Several times I had to walk away from him in order to cope with all that he was throwing at me verbally. I could sympathize with his frustration, but I didn't have an answer and I had made up my mind that I wasn't going to be on the receiving end of his anger any more. Working solo, I realized, as I walked alone along the seafront at Hastings one day, had given me a new independence. I still loved, appreciated and respected Eddie, but now I was on my own more and more, and it was a place I was starting to enjoy.

I should have rejected an offer to do a panto at Hull that year, but, once again, Eddie insisted that he could do it. Was he doing it just for my sake, I wondered, or was it for fear of giving up and then losing everything?

I found myself rushing from one side of the stage to the other, while Eddie stood next to our amplifier centre stage.

Some nights I would hear the audience gasp in surprise as Eddie walked out on stage and leant on the box. As far as I was concerned, part of the visual fun had always been seeing this tubby little man run around the stage, while I, as thin as I am, stood still doing nothing. Now that this crucial dynamic between us had changed, I knew that the act was finished. I was terribly sad that nearly 40 years as a double act was going to come to an end, but it had to be as we were both completely out of breath after every performance and the effort of attempting this several times a day for ten weeks nearly killed Eddie!

'Eddie, you can't go on like this!' I said one day, during the slow short walk from the hotel to the theatre as he clung on to a lamppost to catch his breath. Even getting up the short flight of stairs to the stage door took ages and Derek had to help him get his shoes and socks on because he couldn't bend down. During the show, Eddie had to sit in the wings between his parts – it was too much effort to get back to the dressing room. The stage management put a seat at the side of the stage, which became 'Eddie's bench'. One night, I saw him sitting there with his head in his hands and his eyes closed and I thought, 'This man is dying.' It looked so bad I had tears in my eyes.

Despite the fact that he was the worst he had been for some time, he never missed a single performance. After seeing him on the bench, I was adamant that we did everything to make life easier. We got a taxi to take us to the theatre and back and we stayed together because I was terrified to leave him on his own. If he had collapsed while I wasn't around, I would never have forgiven myself.

As we sat in the hotel's reception area one morning, waiting for our lift, the footballer Lee Bowyer went past. We had seen him a few times, as he was staying at the same hotel. Lee noticed us and smiled, even though he was facing a court case at the time.

'Don't worry mate,' said Eddie, a keen football fan. 'It could be worse. You could be in panto with us!'

Bowyer was acquitted and I suppose we were, too, because it was to be the last panto we did together.

10

OH YES I CAN!

When Eddie called me up to say that he had to have a new heart, I was shocked but not surprised. Another visit to the specialist had resulted in him putting what was virtually a fait accompli to Eddie – he was told that if he didn't have a full heart transplant within the next few months, he would die. He and his wife Patsy had thought about it and decided that they really had no choice. Now it was a case of waiting for a heart to become available.

This news brought with it new and serious questions about the future of Little and Large. Even if Eddie made a full recovery that enabled him to get back on stage, it would be many months or perhaps even years before we could work together again. I was sorry for Eddie and was keen to do all I could to help and support him at this time, but I also had my own life and that of my family to consider. With Little and Large completely out of action, how was I going to earn a living? It was time to ask some tough questions and make some hard decisions.

Sitting around the family dinner table one Sunday evening, having enjoyed another of Sheree's marvellous roasts, I was staring into the flames of our fire with a glass of red wine in my hand and being slowly mesmerized.

'I need a career move,' I heard myself say.

'Kylie Minogue got a new career when she wore those gold hotpants,' quipped Sheree's mum.

'Yes, that's exactly what I need,' I sighed.

A small silence and then:

'So when are you going to start wearing gold hotpants?' asked Mum.

We all fell about laughing, particularly as Mum had said this in all seriousness.

I'm not sure that gold hotpants would have given me the sort of career move I had intended, but at least it started the ball rolling with a laugh. Now, whenever I'm preparing for a theatre job, we have a running joke when I go out of the house: 'Have you got your gold hotpants on, Syd?'

My experiences of little hotel gigs with me and my guitar, coupled with the immense confidence my gospel gigs had given me, were the main driving force behind a new desire to go solo in a more radical way. The question was, where would I start? No agent in their right mind would take on just one half of a comedy double act. Particularly the stooge.

Showbiz has a bad history of double acts trying to go solo. When Eric Morecambe died, Ernie struggled to continue in his own right with not much success, despite being a very clever and talented man. When Mike and Bernie Winters split, their names seemed to completely disappear, even though they both had successful careers in other ways. If they couldn't do it, what chance did I have?

I suppose it was faith that, once again, God would open a door and I'd be given a chance to prove myself. The first step came surprisingly in the form of Chris Gidney. Besides running Christians in Entertainment, Chris is an author and produces touring shows. His father was in the business and Chris spent 12 years in the West End, on tour and with the BBC, so he has an all-round knowledge of how the business works.

In 2002, Chris called me to say that he was producing a new show called 'Night of a Thousand Laughs'. He was bringing Cannon and Ball, Don Maclean and Jimmy Cricket together, along with Charlie the Clown, female vocalist Diane

Regan and some dancers. There was also the Mike Ryal Band. Would I be interested in doing my solo spot?

'What solo spot?' I asked.

'The one you are working on,' he reminded me.

It was a great opportunity to put together a 20-minute act that would work for a commercial audience and would work in my favour, too. In an age where shows were getting smaller and often abandoned the use of dancers and live music, this project was quite unusual. I was a bit worried that Chris would lose out financially with the venture.

As it turned out, the first try-out at St Georges Hall in Bradford was a great success – not only in terms of ticket sales but also with all these comedians on one bill. There was the worry that the audience would be all laughed out by the end, but interspersed with dance, songs and visual effects, the comedy was carried well and Bobby, Tommy, Don and Jimmy were all in their element. The only one who was unsure was me!

The dress rehearsal had been a minor disaster as a petrol strike and serious flooding had made everyone's journey very difficult. Tommy had been trapped leaving his home town of York because of the torrential rain and floods and called from his mobile to say that he might not make it. He eventually arrived just ten minutes before the show, to the great relief of us all – particularly me as Bobby kept looking at me the whole time with a look in his eyes that said, 'Well, you're a stooge, so if Tommy doesn't arrive, let's make it Little and Ball!'

Despite the hindrances, the theatre was full and receptive and Cannon and Ball, Don and Jimmy stormed 'em, as they always do. Then, as Don gave my introduction, my heart was in my mouth.

'Ladies and gentlemen, here, without Eddie Large but with Buddy Holly, is . . . Syd Little!'

I bounced on, picked up my guitar and I was away.

The following 20 minutes were a good test to see if what I had been doing as part of my gospel and small solo gigs would work on the bigger stage. Between songs I told the story of Little and Large in small, bite-sized chunks and the audience roared with laughter. They applauded when I announced that Eddie and I had just celebrated being in showbusiness for 40 years. The interesting thing is that I wasn't really telling gags, but talking about real-life incidents that had happened to me and Eddie over the years. Finishing with that good old 1960s Monkees' song 'I'm a Believer', I left the audience to face the interval.

Backstage, Bobby and Tommy looked surprised and I realized that they hadn't had a clue what I was going to do. Always the jokers and leg pullers that they are, rather than congratulate me, they complained that I had been on stage three minutes longer than I was booked for.

Then it was '. . . Syd, you're stealing our lines because we've been in showbiz for 40 years, too!'

Every time I work with them now, they still make the same complaint. Even if I did 30 seconds, I'm sure they would tell me off, so it's a bit like working with Eddie all over again!

The show went on a short tour the following year and the last night was at the Pavilion Theatre in Bournemouth. To hear nearly a thousand people laughing and clapping was such a joy for us all. We're still waiting for Chris to do it all again.

A stepping stone on from this was when Chris produced a different show called 'A Night with the Stars' and coupled me with the vicar from *Dad's Army*, Frank Williams. It was created around the idea of a Parkinson-style presentation with solo spots and interviews. A small try-out tour was moderately successful and we continued, on and off, until March 2003, but the show never quite pulled the audiences we expected.

We eventually put this down to the fact that perhaps

putting a comic and an actor together confused people who read the bill because they weren't quite sure what they were getting for their money. This theory was perhaps proven when Chris took Frank out on his own in another chat-style production called 'More Tea Vicar?' as the audiences increased dramatically. Like the music business, you don't know whether something will work until you try it. If we knew what songs or shows would be big hits we would all be millionaires.

It was lovely working with Frank Williams. He is such an experienced actor and I enjoyed reading bits of his autobiography, *Vicar to Dad's Army*, while we were touring together. We compared notes about our experiences of working on live television and he never minded my asking him all kinds of questions about one of the classic TV series I love the most.

All these shows were pushing me in the right direction and, above all, proving to myself, audiences and other producers that I had something worthwhile to offer on my own. It also helped confirm that people were still interested to see me and were willing to prove it by buying tickets.

One of the most common comments I got after a show was, 'You are so easy to listen to, Syd. You seem so sincere and genuine, like a friend we have known for years.' 'It's not like you are putting on an act,' said another. 'It's real and what you say comes straight from your heart. We felt like we were the only people in the theatre as you were talking and singing just to us.' 'You're actually a good singer,' said another. 'We like you better on your own.'

Comments like these really helped me to formulate and develop what I did. Even the negative ones were helpful, such as, 'Hi, Syd. I hope you're going to be funny tonight!' from one gentleman as he walked past the stage door.

Someone else who came to see one of my early solo shows said, 'When we were watching you, we were constantly waiting for Eddie to suddenly appear, but there'll come a time when you don't need to mention Eddie as part of your act because you'll be established enough on your own.'

While I appreciated what he was trying to say and that it was meant in a kindly way, I don't think that I could ever ignore the fact that Little and Large has been such a big part of my life. I was discovering that my audiences wanted both old and new material, even if the Little and Large bits are just memories that I recall for theatregoers who are increasingly in need of nostalgia.

This hunger for nostalgia comes from the fact that the popular entertainment programmes we grew up with and enjoyed as families are no longer there. People miss them and, as nothing has replaced them, they love to recall different names and series they enjoyed in the past. People constantly ask me why they don't see me on telly any more.

'Because I can't cook, I'm not a gardener and I'm no good at DIY!' I say.

Actually that last one is a bit of a white lie, but it gets a laugh and sometimes a round of applause because it's so true. Reality TV has replaced pure entertainment, such as the likes of The Two Ronnies, Val Doonican, Russ Abbott and others who are simply not around on our screens any more. The truth is, though, that the people who watched those shows still are – a fact proved recently when I met Les Want while on another tour with Cannon and Ball.

Les is best known for his appearances in the famous *The Black and White Minstrel Show*. It was interesting timing, because I had just performed two spots for a Minstrel-based show that had done a short northern tour. It was quite fun, but all the singers and dancers were young and inexperienced and I was quite keen to hear what Les had to say about the original show.

As I sat in a café in Leicester with Chris, Les told how, despite being on television for nearly 30 years and winning many of the top awards, the show was suddenly removed from our screens.

'The audiences that loved it must still be there, though.'

As Chris listened, I could see a familiar twinkle forming in his eyes, around which was swirling the steam of a cappuccino.

'Let's bring the show back to the stage,' he said. Chris had already had a small and moderately successful season with Les down in Devon the previous summer, with a show in which Les had played tribute to that great entertainer Al Jolson.

'There's no need to black up because that's out of date and the music, medleys and costumes are the most important part,' surmised Chris as he thought aloud. In that little café, 'Memories of the Minstrels' was born.

After discovering some of the original costumes and luring stars of the series such as Margaret Savage to appear alongside Les, it went on to a sell-out first night and a very successful tour.

Chris, who co-produces the tour with its Musical Director Michael Wooldridge, told me that, on the first night, in the curtain speech at the end of the show, Les was choking back the tears as he said, 'Tonight has been the first time I have sung with Maggie for 28 years!'

Ironically, a few weeks later, they got a call from the BBC to say that they were filming a documentary about the series and asking if they would like to be involved. They were also going to repeat one of the last programmes. Well, I'm still waiting for a similar call from the BBC saying that they are going to repeat *The Little & Large Show*!

In the meantime, I was determined to bring back some good old-fashioned popular entertainment in my own way, but, in my attempts to become re-established as a solo performer, I wanted to be taken seriously. It wasn't fame I was chasing – I had already achieved that and, even after being off the box for nearly ten years, people still recognized me on the street and in restaurants. No, it was more the desire to continue performing and earning a living from what I enjoy doing best. In effect, this took all the sting and panic out of the journey for me. I could just let things happen at their own pace and watch as each new door opened.

A local comedian called Tony Jo suggested that his agency ring me to ask if I could support the Grumbleweeds for six weekends at Southport. Graham, who looks like Charlie Drake, and Robin, the tall one who always dresses up in the most amazing costumes, were great fun to work with. Robin was forever telling me off for doing gags, implying that it was hard to follow, but they are such a superbly polished comedy duo that there was never any question of them falling flat.

Not long afterwards, I found myself supporting Joe Longthorne at the North Pier, Blackpool. This is where we did our first summer season as Little and Large. Ironically, Eddie had been ill with a stomach bug during that season! On the bill had been Norman Collier, Jim Davidson and Frank Carson. Now it was just me supporting Joe alongside brilliant comics such as Johnny Casson. Would my own showbiz family believe in me?

I didn't want to let Joe Longthorne down. We had worked with him on many occasions and knew him well. I also knew that the first five rows of the audience would not only be full of Joe's fans, but would be the same people at every performance. How would they react to me?

'Don't be afraid,' said Joe as we stood in the wings on the first night. Perhaps he had heard my teeth chattering or knees knocking again. 'Be confident.'

It was good advice. I knew that if I went out on stage showing nerves, it would make the audience anxious and create a barrier that would be hard to overcome. I remembered the confidence I had with the gospel gigs and took a deep breath.

Joe introduced me, which was a real privilege as it sort of underlined that my showbiz friends really did have faith in me.

As the weekends went on, Joe's fans would collar me after the show and say things like, 'The act is great, Syd. We can see you're getting more confident!' It was strange to have such professional comments come from an audience, but I suppose they had seen plenty of acts in their time following Joe around!

The only thing that I couldn't do was my Gene Pitney because Joe did that, but at least I had gathered enough material by then to put in something else. The fact that I told the Little and Large story, interspersed with relevant gags and songs, was seen as quite unique. Nobody else was standing in front of an audience telling their own story in this way.

Johnny Casson was particularly encouraging to me in developing this whole idea as I began to tread the old familiar boards alone.

'When you talk about your first season here with all those stars,' he suggested, 'why don't you bring it up to date with a gag like . . . "In fact, I saw Jim Davidson the other day and he asked me if I could lend him 20 pence to phone his ex-wife. I said, 'Here, have a quid and phone them all!'"' It's unusual for a comic to give away good material, but Johnny Casson was very generous.

Tony Peers is a comedian who also produces a lot of shows for the Butlin's Hotel circuit as well as the Spa Theatre in Scarborough. He had heard that I was working solo and offered me a long summer season there in 2003. This time, I was to be a compere and link all the different acts together, as well as doing my own spots.

On the Monday it was a Minstrel show, Tuesday was olde time music hall, and Wednesday was a summer spectacular. I had to have three different acts to match the different shows throughout the week.

One night, I was being heckled constantly by a guy sitting at the side who was obviously the worse for wear. I battled on as best I could and eventually pulled out a line to deal with him: 'Hey, mate. I can see why you're sitting near the wall, 'cos that's plastered too!'

It's unlike me to be anything but gentle in my comedy, but this was the right time and the right place and it worked a treat. I am acutely aware that trying to deal with a heckler might also open a can of worms. It's best not to jump straight in because, nine times out of ten, once a heckler starts enjoying the attention, there is no stopping him – and it is usually a 'him'. The only thing that the performer has over the heckler is the mic, but sometimes even this is not enough to bring serious interruptions to a halt. I've seen some acts who have been destroyed by a heckler they tried to take on. I've even seen audiences walk out and ask for their money back. I always advise that it's better to ignore them for as long as possible, hope the audience does, too, and, eventually, they'll give up.

It's also crucial that a performer never alienates the audience. I always remember a story that I was told when I first went into the business about how not to deal with a difficult crowd. The legendary Dickie Henderson's dad was standing in the wings watching his son perform in the late 1950s. Things were obviously not going to plan because his dad could hear Dickie starting to get more and more frustrated with the audience.

'What are you drinking out there, cement?' and 'I've never performed for dead people before' were some of the things that he was throwing out into the darkness.

As soon as Dickie came off stage, his dad hit him.

'What's that for, Dad?'

'That audience didn't know they were a bad audience until you told them!'

So, never put your audience down. Even the master heckler

manager, Jim Davidson, mentioned me in his book, saying I never really got the chance to shine.

Jim was to have a big effect on my career. I got a call from Johnny Martin to ask if I would appear in one of Jim's pantomime productions in Sunderland. After a year off from panto, in which I enjoyed my sixtieth birthday and some unexpected time with family and friends, I missed something that had been part of my working life for nearly 40 years. My birthday normally coincided with the opening night of pantomime each year and, in a funny sort of way, having a normal life at Christmas seemed very strange.

I was to appear with Darren Day and Jean Fergusson at the Empire. A photo call in London, with me wearing my red and white costume, was great fun – particularly when the photographer, who was high up on a ladder looking down on me, toppled and nearly fell off. I was getting ready to catch him when the flash went. This was the cause of the surprised laugh on my face in the picture that ended up on advertising posters all over Sunderland.

As I left the photo shoot, I had another laugh when I bumped into Joe Pasquale in the street. He was also doing a pantomime for Jim, but somewhere else, and was fascinated to hear that this would be my first ever solo pantomime. I was both chuffed to bits and scared stiff. It was one thing doing a solo spot as part of a show, it was quite another working as a close-knit team on something as specialized as pantomime.

Arriving at the theatre for rehearsal later that year, I was greeted like some long-lost uncle by all the cast. They had grown up with me on television and considered me to be a seasoned panto performer. I suppose I was, and I did feel quite like a veteran when Darren Day said, 'Syd, I used to watch you every Saturday night when I was a small boy.' Not only did it make me feel very old, but shocked me as

I thought about the impact that Little and Large had had on several generations.

Most pantomime scripts are quite threadbare when it comes to comedy lines and whoever is the laughter-maker in the show is expected to throw in several gags of their own. As I was playing Baron Hardup, there was an even greater lack of gags because this is a role that is often played by a straight actor. So, after the first night nerves were well and truly over, I started adding some of my own material. That Christmas, there was a lovely advert with the wonderful Julie Walters playing a fairy in a supermarket. So, when Jean Fergusson, from *Last of the Summer Wine*, came on dressed as Fairy Godmother, I shouted out, 'Where are you from, Asda?' It brought the house down and Jean was laughing so much that the pumpkin carriage was delayed for a moment or two.

When Darren was off sick for a few days with a terrible dose of laryngitis, it didn't faze me at all. 'Alone again, naturally,' I sang to myself in my little dressing room in the words of Gilbert O'Sullivan.

Darren and I normally did the songsheet routine together, but with Darren off, I was soon in my element. This is where, at the end of the show, the theatre ushers choose several of the younger members of the audience to come on stage to have a little competition to see who can sing the best. I had already learned very quickly what *not* to ask the tiny volunteers.

'Have you come with your mum and dad?'

'No, we haven't got a dad, just an Uncle John', came the little reply.

'Have you had a good Christmas?' I asked another.

'We don't celebrate Christmas. We're Jehovah's Witnesses,' exclaimed the child.

A popular gag at the end of the songsheet is for me to pretend to leave one child out. I give all the others a bag of sweets apart from one, then wait for the audience to shout out something appropriate like, 'What about the one who's behind you?' When I did this with one little boy, though, he suddenly burst into tears and I felt dreadful. Before I could do anything, one of the other children, a little girl, rushed on stage and said, 'It's OK, you can have mine!' It killed my gag but the whole audience melted.

Another little lad was nervous from the word go. As I started to interview him, I could see that he was shaking.

'Hello, what's your name?' I enquired as gently as I could. No reply.

'Where are you from?'

No reply. He wouldn't even look me in the face and I wondered if I should give up and move on then and there or keep trying. Suddenly I saw a flow of water appear swiftly out of a trouser leg and run down over his shoe.

'Oh dear,' I whispered. 'You'd better go back to your mum.'

I was wondering what the members of the orchestra were going to do when faced with the little stream of liquid that was about to appear over their heads. One of my eyes watched them move their sheet music and the other was on the boy.

'Bye then,' I said, but the little chap wouldn't move. He was fixed to the spot as if someone had nailed him to the stage. I realized that despite the little accident, he wasn't going to shift until he got his goodie bag. That was what he had come for and, even though his nerves and his bladder had let him down, he wasn't going to be robbed of the ultimate prize. I rushed off stage, grabbed the plastic bag of chocolates and returned to see his little face light up like a new bulb. As I picked him up and carried him to the steps leading down into the auditorium, he got the biggest round of applause and the loudest 'aahhhh!' I have ever heard.

The drama carried on as I continued with the other children

and one of the girl dancers came on with a mop. You can't really come on and wipe a stage in front of a packed audience very surreptitiously, but it didn't help when she slipped on the wet floor and let out a little squeak of horrified surprise. At least one poor dancer slipping was better than the whole company doing so during the final moments of the show when they came on to take a bow.

The next night couldn't have been any more different. How do the ushers manage to pick them! When the time came for the songsheet, at the back of the little line of small figures winding their way forward was a kid whose very walk suggested that he was the kid from hell. As soon as he made it to the stage, he became an immediate attention grabber. Shouting into the mic, pinching the little girl next to him and stamping his feet, he had the audience mesmerized. I was starting to try to think on my feet, but when he began to run off stage and round the back of the curtain with the next scene's props in his hands, I knew I had a problem.

Of course, the audience were on his side because he was causing such havoc that it was making them laugh and they wanted to see what I was going to do about it. Even when he moved over and stood on my foot, I had to smile sweetly. By this time he was the last child on stage and he was due his goodies. I could see from a certain glint in his eye that I wasn't going to get rid of him that easily. When I put a book across his arms to act as a tray for all the other goodies to come, he just dropped it on the floor. I picked it up and we started again. This time I managed to pile a lot of chocolate on top before he once again decided to drop the whole lot on the floor. I patiently recovered all the goodies and we started again, only to reach the last item before the entire lot was deposited everywhere once again. The members of the audience, who had been falling about with laughter up until now, suddenly decided that they had had enough. They didn't like this five-year-old any more and were willing me to give him the biggest telling off the poor kid had ever had in his life.

The last straw came after a final attempt to keep him still had succeeded and I had handed him a story tape. He dropped the whole armful once again and proceeded to pull the brown tape out from the cassette case. By now the audience was actually booing him off. I was still bent over picking up all the items he had thrown around the stage and into the pit when I saw this lovely pair of bare legs walk past me. I straightened up to see this beautiful blonde woman standing beside me. As soon as she picked up the little boy, he changed. No longer was he the kid from planet Zog, but the sweetest little child you could have imagined.

'Hello, are you his mum?'

'Indeed I am not!' came the stiff reply. 'I am the au pair.'

In all my years of appearing on stage, with plenty of unexpected things happening, it was the strangest and scariest event I have ever witnessed.

After the show, I still didn't stop singing. The cast would often disappear down to the local club where the karaoke would play all night. I once got up and sang for three hours with my guitar and no one seemed bored. Perhaps I should have passed a hat around afterwards or maybe I should have become a busker.

It was a great season and I must have shined enough for Jim because I was invited back for another pantomime the following year.

When I was booked for a two-week cruise for the Fred Olson Line I knew what to expect as Eddie and I had done many of these shows over the years, but I was still very nervous. On the first day, I sat in my cabin and peered out of the porthole and wondered how long it would take me to swim back home!

It's usual to only do two or three spots during the fortnight, so the rest of the time is your own. Cruises are a lovely mixture of work and relaxation, but, for some performers, the downside is that you are always on duty. Apart from shutting yourself in your cabin all day, there's nowhere you can hide.

'Hi, Syd. What are you singing tonight?' would be a regular question as I sat on the sun deck reading the newspaper or grabbing 40 winks. It really didn't bother me as I have always been a people person who, as Sheree says, would talk to anyone, even dead people.

The ship is called the *Black Watch*, and has a swimming pool, a fitness centre, health and beauty salon, deck sports, library, indoor games, Internet access, casino and a 150-seat theatre. What more could anyone want?

My only problem was providing the band with my music. When I walked out on stage for my afternoon band call, I chit-chatted away as I always do and thought that they were really unfriendly because they hardly looked up from their instruments. It wasn't until the Musical Director spoke that I realized they were Russian and hadn't understood a word. When they began to play my music, however, it was like singing with the Hallé Orchestra.

Perhaps by now I was getting a bit too cocky because I was agreeing to almost any work that was offered. So, when a request came for an after-dinner speaking engagement, I took on the challenge without a thought. I didn't even check my diary properly, so, as the time approached, I was horrified to see that I had virtually double booked myself. I was appearing at the Assembly Hall Theatre at Tunbridge Wells as part of a three-day comedy tour and due at the Pavilion Theatre, Bournemouth, the next day. In between these two dates, I now had to travel up to Leeds for the lunchtime after-dinner event and back down to Bournemouth for that evening. I considered asking Don Maclean, who I was touring with at the time, if I could borrow his private plane, but decided I would look very silly. He probably hadn't brought it with him anyway!

After the show, I drove through the night to Leeds. Consequently, when I eventually stood up to deliver my speech, I was half asleep. The booker said it was a mixed, older type of crowd, which is my audience, but, when I got there, the tables were full of young people and they were all male. I doubted if some of them even knew who Little and Large were.

By the time I began to speak, several were pretty drunk and, to make matters worse, it was the first day of the World Cup. Huge screens behind me were projecting the build-up in front of a jeering group of men who, I am sure, didn't want to listen to me. I was filling the gap between soup and the main course and had to finish by the time the match was officially supposed to start.

As I stood there facing this mass of male bodies, I began to shake in my shoes so much that I wouldn't have been surprised if they had fallen off altogether.

'Hiya, my name is Syd Little. Hands up all those who thought we were dead?'

An opening line that normally gets a big laugh was met with complete silence. I could hear my knees starting to knock together as the rest of my patter got a similar response and I soon started to feel a huge wall of doubt begin to slowly descend within me. I was dying on my feet and didn't think I would last 5 minutes, let alone the 20 allotted.

A loud cynical snigger from a nearby table threw me completely and the whole situation caused a sense of doom to start eating away inside me. Somehow I reached the allocated time and sank to my seat accompanied by some half-hearted applause from my own table. 'Well, if anyone wants the video of that, just let me know!' was the sarcastic comment that followed.

If there was ever a time when I wanted the ground to open up and swallow me, this was it. I had to endure the next hour of embarrassment as I ate main course, dessert and coffee. As I drove all the way back to Bournemouth, I vowed I would never attempt anything like that ever again.

All the guys in the show asked how it had gone and I told them I had died. They told me that I mustn't give up, which was just as well, because that is exactly what had been going through my head. However, as Sir Harry Secombe once said, 'Every comedian needs a disaster, it makes you more street-wise.' When I got out on stage with a band behind me and a packed house laughing at my gags, I felt redeemed once more.

After the awful experience of the after-dinner speech, I felt that I really needed someone to field the enquiries properly and help keep my diary in order. I certainly didn't want to go back to being a puppet – I was really enjoying my new-found independence – but the telephone was now starting to ring on a regular basis and booking gigs and negotiating fees is a specialist field. I was now entering a new marketplace, taking me from the small cabaret shows at hotels to proper theatres, but I avoided after-dinner speeches!

Peter Pritchard, who had looked after us as Little and Large, wasn't really interested in taking me on alone. His parting words on the telephone were, 'It's a jungle out there, Syd. You get what you can and it's all right by me.'

To be honest, I wasn't that keen on having one agent – I didn't want to keep all my eggs put in one basket any more. My first thoughts were to go through an old mate of mine, little Johnny Martin and his wife Chris, because he had shown faith in taking Little and Large on in the early days. I call him 'little' Johnny Martin because he's quite short and I love him for that – it's not every day that I find someone who is smaller than me!

I've known him for years, so I rang him to let him know that I was now going solo, and he said, 'I would love to take you on, Syd.'

He was intrigued with the idea of getting one half of a

double act some work, but said that he would test the waters. Initially he had a lot of booking agents say that they knew what Little and Large did, but what did Syd do on his own? It was difficult for Johnny to explain until he got an emergency call one day in May from Thompson Holidays. They had been let down and wanted to know who else Johnny had available. He mentioned my name and there was silence at the other end of the phone.

'Why don't you give him a chance?' suggested Johnny and the booker agreed.

'Syd, they want you to fly out to Corfu to one of their Thompson Gold hotels and do two spots,' said Johnny. 'Can you manage that?'

'When do they want me to go?'

'Tomorrow!' was his reply.

I arrived at Manchester Airport's reception desk, bleary eyed, a few hours later with bags packed and guitar over my shoulder. I never let the guitar go in the luggage hold because I'm always scared it will be thrown around and inadvertently broken. It's worth quite a lot and more fragile than people think. Without my original 1960s Fender I'm lost. I bought it when we had The Shadows on our TV show and even Hank Marvin said it was a good 'un.

I asked for my ticket at the desk, half wondering if it was all some sort of bluff, but a smile and some paperwork came in my direction and I was soon up in the skies. My body wasn't the only thing that was up in the air, though – my stomach was too. The lady at the desk had insisted that my guitar go in the hold, so I was having kittens all the way in case it arrived with a broken neck. Added to this, I was unusually worried because I had never done anything like this before – not even with Eddie.

A few hours later, I felt a blast of hot air as I stepped out of the plane and on to the tarmac. I held my breath as I waited for my guitar to appear on the baggage reclaim belt.

To my great relief it was still in one piece and, as I stepped on to the link coach from the airport to hotel, I heard the familiar, 'Hi, Syd. What are ya doin' here? Are you entertaining us?' It was like being at home even though I was in a different country. It helped calm my nerves a little, but I had to wait a few days before I could do my solo spot.

The hotel manager and Thompson reps were all very friendly and showed me the cabaret stage where I would be performing. I was amazed at the state-of-the-art equipment they had, from complicated stage lighting to a seriously good PA system. The thing was, it was all outdoors.

The next day, as soon as I stepped out on to the open-air stage, I could feel that these people were my type of audience. The welcome was lovely and to sing some of my favourite songs under a starry sky and chat to a very relaxed audience for an hour was oh so nice.

As I sat by the pool the next day, exposed to what the audience might say to me, everyone was giving me the thumbs up. The only odd thing was an ever-flowing demand for photographs with me. Odd because it didn't seem to matter what state of dress or undress I was in, people still wanted one. There must be hundreds of pictures with me with my little shorts and sunglasses on, smiling out from photos all over England. Seeing me in shorts, people were amused at how thin I really am. I haven't yet developed a middle- or even later-aged spread, much to the annoyance of those around me who have.

I also had a few 'Glad to see you're better!' comments as people confused me with Eddie and 'I thought you'd have retired ages ago, the money you and Eddie made!' I've always found it silly to contradict people who might come up and say they saw us at Bournemouth in 1979 when I knew it was Daley and Wayne or Cannon and Ball they were talking about. It's the same when they think I'm a millionaire, I don't believe it's necessary to take away the illusion, because it only spoils it for them. Part of the fun of showbiz is the fantasy and glamour of it all.

So, my first visit to Corfu went down well and word was sent back that I was 'good'. Not just 'all right', but 'good'. I was pleased with that and wasn't so surprised when I was invited back for a whole new string of dates, though I went out and bought a cheap guitar before I flew again rather than risk my precious Fender having less luck this time!

11

A CHANGE OF HEART

An invitation to appear on a special *This is Your Life* in late 2002 about Bob Monkhouse was greeted by Eddie and me with open arms. We loved and admired Bob, who shared the same agent, Peter Pritchard, as us.

When we arrived at the studio and took our places in the specially designated area to help spring the surprise, Michael Aspel, the show's host, came over to us. I could see the shock on his face as he took one look at Eddie and noticed how ill my pal looked. Sheree and Patsy, Eddie's wife, have always got on well and were chatting away to each other as normal. I was just so worried about Eddie and anxious when I saw so many people giving him second glances.

The evening went well and Bob got the surprise and accolades he deserved. After a short after-show reception, Sheree and Patsy hugged goodbye and I shook Eddie's hand. On the way home, I confessed to Sheree that I had this awful feeling that it was going to be the last time I would see him.

Several months later, Sheree got a call to say that Eddie had suddenly been admitted to hospital in Bristol, near their home, and that it didn't look too good. A further call confirmed that they were unable to help him there and that he was now being rushed by ambulance to Papworth Hospital, 174 miles away. I looked at Sheree as she put the phone down and, as our eyes met, they seemed to say the same thing. Again we wondered whether he would survive the four-hour emergency journey.

Sheree and I decided that we should get in the car and go to be with them, whatever the situation. Some 230 miles later, we arrived at the hospital, only to discover that Eddie hadn't yet arrived. Patsy, his son and two daughters, were waiting in another room. We tried not to fear the worst when the doors suddenly swung open and in came Eddie on the steel trolley. Sheree and I were therefore the first to see him, so we went straight over to try to bring him some comfort from seeing our familiar faces.

'Hi, Eddie,' I said, in as cheerful a voice as I could muster.

I held his hand as they wheeled him into the ward and was struck by how very cold he was to the touch. Eddie looked as white as the blankets that covered him and was shaking uncontrollably. This caused all the attached tubes and wires around him to join in the shuddering, creating a most peculiar sight.

'Would you mind leaving now?' said a consultant in a white coat, gently.

We reluctantly turned away and left Eddie to the experts. On the way out, we bumped into Patsy, her son and the girls.

'He's in safe hands,' I said, trying to bring some consolation to Eddie's understandably distressed wife.

'They told me his kidneys were starting to fail,' explained Patsy. 'They said he may have less than 24 hours to live, unless they can do something.'

We sat down and chatted over several cups of tea in the hospital café.

'Are they going to do a transplant now?' I gently enquired.

'No, they can only do that when one becomes available. They are just trying to stabilize him with drugs and fluids to try to halt his deterioration,' explained Patsy.

An hour or so later, a serious-looking nurse slowly approached us. We immediately fell silent, hoping not to hear the inevitable.

'Would you like to follow me?' she said. 'Eddie's ready to see you.'

We couldn't quite believe what we were hearing – I nearly asked the nurse to repeat herself. The nurse led us back into the ward, where Eddie was now sitting up in bed, looking as bright as a button. I wanted to ask Sheree to pinch me, because I was sure this was all a dream. How could he have made such a quick recovery from being at what seemed to be death's door? The skill of paramedics, doctors and nurses still amazes me and it was their incredible abilities that had not only saved Eddie's life, but put him back on track as well.

Sheree and I said goodbye to Eddie, Patsy and the children and drove back to Blackpool. The reassurance that Eddie was still alive filled us with great hope, but we also had the knowledge that it was not yet over. Eddie still desperately needed a heart transplant and this thought still hung in our minds like a black cloud as the miles sped by.

A few days later, we heard that Eddie was now back at home, recuperating from the kidney failure, and that he was now at the top of the list when a suitable heart became available.

A few weeks went by and then we had another surprise call from Patsy to tell us that Eddie was now the proud owner of a new heart. New to him, that is – it had actually belonged to someone else beforehand, but, because of their generosity and sacrifice and that of their relatives, Eddie now had the opportunity to start a new life.

Most donor hearts have to be transplanted within four to six hours, so there was little time to lose and he had already had his bags packed at home in readiness for such a call. All the tests showed that this heart was suitable and, after a very long operation, he was resting in the hospital bed, breathing normally by himself.

I wondered what difference it would make to the way Eddie viewed his own life now. Living on borrowed time? Indebted to someone else's big-heartedness, literally! I'm looking forward to perhaps reading his own book one day where he will give us the full story.

I was told that Papworth is the country's main heart and lung transplantation centre. The service began in 1979 with the first successful heart transplant by Sir Terence English. Their first successful heart and lung transplant was carried out in 1984, followed by the first heart, lung and liver transplant in the world in October 1986. Since 1991, all types of cardiopulmonary transplants have been carried out, including both single and double lung operations, so really Eddie couldn't have been in a better place.

We all held our breath and I sent up plenty of prayers for Eddie as he remained on the critical list. After three days, he was moved to a ward with others recovering from similar major operations and, after nearly a fortnight, was to spend a further week or so in the intermediate discharge flat in Papworth village, where the experts prepared him for the move back to his own home and community.

In the summer of 2003, two weeks after his operation, and following a gospel gig in the West Country, I drove across to see him on my way home. I wondered what I would discover when I arrived at the hospital, only to find that his bed was empty.

'Hi, Syd!' came the voice from a nearby chair. There was Eddie, now out of bed, in his everyday clothes, looking more like his normal self than I had seen in several years!

'Eddie, you're looking fantastic!' We sat and chatted for a while and I asked what those other half a dozen men walking around with tubes were in for.

'Oh they're all heart transplants,' he said nonchalantly.

'You're joking!'

I always thought that heart transplants were rare things, but I now know that Papworth's heart and lung transplant programme carries out about 66 transplants a year, so it's quite a usual thing for them, something they do every week.

I chatted to one man who had been called to the hospital on seven occasions, only to find each time that the heart was not compatible. Eddie had been very lucky.

As I made my way back home, I was eager to tell Sheree what I had seen and what a miracle had been performed. As I drove near to our street, I glimpsed that well-known poster advertising guide dogs for the blind. 'Great double acts!' it announces in its title with a picture of Little and Large alongside a man and his dog. Even with Eddie now looking like he was going to make a full recovery, I wondered if we would still remain together.

Several months later, in March 2004, I received an extraordinary telephone call from someone asking me if I would be interested in auditioning for the West End musical *Chitty Chitty Bang Bang*. It was certainly interesting timing because I had been to see the show while staying with Chris and his family in London the previous year. I was quite knocked out by the pace and spectacle of the show with its wonderful flying car.

I agreed to come down to London and talk about the possibilities, though I was quite unsure about the practicalities of the idea as I already had a busy diary for the year ahead. Not only would it involve cancelling all these dates, but did I really want to live away from home for a year? Even with these serious questions in my mind, I thought it would be fun to find out what was being suggested and, if nothing else, would just let people know I was happy to try anything in my new career!

After a late night curry at Chris' house, I made the early morning train journey to Victoria Station and then caught a taxi to Piccadilly. It seemed that all the numbers down this long, famous street were very higgledy piggledy because even the taxi driver couldn't work out which building I should be going to. A bit like the character I'm thinking of playing, I thought to myself. The producers had asked me to come and talk about the role of Grandpa Potts, which was being played by the wonderful Russ Abbott. A strange, bumbling, quirky character, greatly loved by his grandchildren. Perfect for me, I thought.

The taxi driver eventually gave up and deposited me outside a Russian airline building, suggesting I walk back the way we had come. As I did so, the wind shot down the street like in a wind tunnel and, after having found the address, I quickly stepped out of the cold into a nearby café. It happened to be the Hard Rock Café and so I felt right at home, with all the guitars hanging on the walls and the drum kit sitting on a shelf above my head. An old Rolling Stones video was on a TV screen and I sang along, reminding myself that, as part of the private audition to follow, I also had to sing.

Refreshed after a frothy cappuccino, I made my way back to the tall, stately building next door and pressed the bell.

'Syd Little for *Chitty Chitty, Bang Bang*,' I said into the intercom, feeling slightly silly. As the huge door swung open, I entered a large hallway with marble on the floors, huge black leather sofas at the sides and gilt-framed James Bond posters on the walls.

The receptionist gave me a huge grin and made a call to let them know I had arrived.

'Why the James Bond posters?' I enquired as I waited.

'This is the London headquarters of the Broccoli family who make all the films,' he explained. I remembered that they are also the producers for *Chitty Chitty Bang Bang*. 'Dad-in-law would have liked to have seen this,' I thought to myself as I gazed at the posters displaying Bond's many acts of heroism.

'There's a cinema downstairs where they invited the last cast of *Chitty* to see a private screening of the latest Bond film,' he offered.

A pleasantly dressed girl appeared and handed me a script. 'Would you mind acquainting yourself with this before we see you?' she asked.

I was happy to do so and read the funny lines on offer. A

few minutes later and I was whisked into a huge drawing
room and was greeted by several others, including the director and producer of the show. Seated at a piano in the corner
was a relaxed-looking pianist. 'He won't look so calm when
he realizes what I'm going to ask him to play,' I chuckled to
myself.

In order to be able to show off my comic, as well as my
vocal skills, I had chosen a song from the Monty Python
movie *The Meaning of Life*. It was also a great test for my
memory skills. I handed the music to the pianist, who took
one look and smirked. 'At least he knows it,' I thought. A few
opening bars and I launched straight into the 'Galaxy Song':

Just remember that you're standing on a planet that's
*   evolving*
And revolving at nine hundred miles an hour,
That's orbiting at nineteen miles a second, so it's
*   reckoned,*
A sun that is the source of all our power.
The sun and you and me and all the stars that we can
*   see*
Are moving at a million miles a day
In an outer spiral arm, at forty thousand miles an hour,
Of the galaxy we call the 'Milky Way'.

Our galaxy itself contains a hundred billion stars.
It's a hundred thousand light years side to side.
It bulges in the middle, sixteen thousand light years
*   thick,*
But out by us, it's just three thousand light years wide.
We're thirty thousand light years from galactic central
*   point.*
We go 'round every two hundred million years,
And our galaxy is only one of millions of billions
In this amazing and expanding universe.

The universe itself keeps on expanding and expanding
In all of the directions it can whizz
As fast as it can go, at the speed of light, you know,
Twelve million miles a minute, and that's the fastest
    speed there is.
So remember, when you're feeling very small and
    insecure,
How amazingly unlikely is your birth,
And pray that there's intelligent life somewhere up in
    space,
*'Cause there's ****** all down here on Earth!*

By the time I had finished, the whole room was literally falling about laughing. One chap was holding himself up against the wall, roaring away. I don't think that they had seen anything else like it before and, in fact, I understand that they had seen a string of well-known actors all morning singing straight songs and so they said it was a complete diversion for them. Complete disaster for them more like!

After delivering a few lines from the script, they thanked me for coming and I left them all with huge smiles on their faces. For me, it was a great fun exercise, but a few days later I got a call from my office to say that they had liked what they saw, and although I wasn't right for the Grandfather part, they would keep me in mind for future shows. So who knows, you might see me in the West End yet.

Back home and I switched on the telly just in time to see Eddie making a surprise appearance. Presenters Des and Mel were asking about his experiences and health while promoting some bits of impersonations he was doing on comedian John Colshaw's new series. I was sad that, throughout the interview, Eddie didn't mention Little and Large once. Others also noticed and mentioned this. I understand how he may want to distance himself from our double act to prove that there is life beyond it, but it was such a fundamental part of our lives for so long, it must be difficult to ignore it completely.

Eddie and I have had a lot of laughs in our lives and career and I hope that, somehow, this will continue. Perhaps not at the same pace, but a special appearance with Eddie now and again would be lovely.

People sometimes ask me, 'If you were to live your life over again, would you change anything?' I have to say 'No, because the good times and the bad times have lived with me side by side and have been of equal value in differing ways. I'm content that, in all I've been through, God had me in his hands and still does. It's almost as if nothing will faze me now because of this. My faith is extremely important to me, as I'm sure you've realized by now! I've heard a lot about the Alpha course, which has become so popular because it explains the basic facts of Christianity to people who just want to know without being pressurized in any way. Unfortunately, I've never been able to go on it because I've never been in one place long enough! However, on plenty of long car journeys, I have listened to the tapes and I love the bit when the creator of the course, Nicky Gumbel, tells the story of watching the 1966 World Cup on the telly. He explains how the picture was all fuzzy – so much so that he really couldn't see where the ball was going. Frustrated, he was almost at breaking point when someone walked into the room and noticed that the aerial was missing. Once this was plugged in, the picture was perfect. That's exactly like me. After all that I have been through, I really don't want to go it alone – I need God to continue to help me through little by little and keep the picture clear.

I always expected others in the business to laugh at me because of my faith, but most people's reactions are positive, once they realize that I'm not going to preach at them! I've found that the best way to talk about my faith among my friends and colleagues is actually to be silent. It's then that people I meet or work with can ask their own questions in their òwn time and in their own way without fear of me coming out with a load of religious jargon – or Godspeak as I call it.

When people hear about what I have been through, and how my faith has played an integral part in this, some are quite jealous. 'I wish I could have your faith, Syd!' they say. I try to explain that it's not so much to do with how much faith I have, it's more to do with just letting God do it all, but this seems too simplistic for them. I suppose we are terribly suspicious of anything we get for free. We are much more comfortable with the idea of having worked and earnt something, so I suspect that many of my showbiz friends would be happier if they had to work their way to heaven, but it just doesn't happen like that.

I know that many people in the business are no longer scared to admit to being a Christian. There are many who have found that faith is essential and are willing to stand up and say so. During the pantomime this year, a dancer came up to me in the wings and said, 'Syd, are you a Christian?'

'Yes!' I said. A few years ago, I would have stumbled over my words, not knowing quite what to say, but the fact is that I'm now very proud to be one. There are plenty more in my profession, though, who are very intrigued and want to know more about the Christian faith, but are sometimes afraid to ask. Chris Gidney and Christians in Entertainment certainly have their work cut out! I know that Chris particularly likes to do what I call a 'Nicodemus'. This was a man in the Bible who used to come and meet Jesus in the middle of the night to talk because he was afraid of what his friends would say if they knew. Chris meets lots of people in the profession in secret because some are afraid that, if they meet in public, it will be all over the newspapers before they have had time to think things through for themselves.

Working alongside Chris is a wonderful lady called Sally

Goring. She runs the Christians in Entertainment prayer line, which anyone in the business can call day or night and know that they will be prayed for in complete confidence. She was also in cahoots with me and a lot of other people for a surprise party for the twentieth anniversary of Christians in Entertainment.

Chris was the only one who didn't know about this and we all went to great lengths to make sure that it was kept a closely guarded secret. As you know, my nickname is Loose Lips Little, so, every time I met or worked with Chris, I was terrified of saying something that would let the cat out of the bag. I think Chris sensed this at times, for occasionally he gave me a few strange looks. Mind you, so do a lot of other people!

The idea for the party was concocted by a lovely man called Lindsey Bennett. I had worked with Lindsey a few times when he joined us as a support act for some of my gospel evenings. Lindsey told me that he had a problem with his name because every time he turned up for a gig, the organizer and audience were always surprised because they thought that they had booked a woman.

'It happens even when I tell them it's a "Lin" with an "i" not a "y",' he explained.

Apart from Chris' unhelpful suggestion that Lin tried wearing a skirt to his gigs, I mentioned that perhaps Lin could simply use a stage name. The problem with that was that Chris, as he has known Lin for such a long time, kept introducing him by his real name, not the one on the posters. It just served to confuse the audience all the more, but provided something for me to chuckle over while waiting to go on stage.

In the meantime, Lin was busy crafting the CIE underground party and it had involved enormous effort, but all seemed to be working to plan, he confided. In the spring, Chris had received a telephone call from Roger Bruce, Cliff

Richard's personal assistant, to say that Chris and his wife
Trinity were invited to a surprise birthday party for Cliff in
November, so could he make sure to keep his diary clear.
Chris, used to the secretive side of the business, took this in
his stride, but was apparently quite frustrated at not knowing
who else was going to be there. A cautious attempt at trying
to get some helpful information from Gill Snow at Cliff's
office only resulted in even more secrecy.

'Sorry, I can't give you a guest list,' Gill told him. 'It's all
so hush-hush and you know how easily things can get out!'

That November, Sheree and I arrived at the hotel in
Sheffield where Cliff was enjoying a day off during a very
long and exhausting UK tour, which was to be followed by
a world tour the following year. I was impressed that Cliff
had agreed to give up a very precious day of rest to be part
of the surprise, but I knew that he had been an encourager
of Chris' work for many years so wouldn't have wanted to
miss it.

There were plenty of other faces among the 40 or so secret
guests there that I knew. Wendy Craig, Russell Boulter, who
was appearing as a nasty piece of work in *Casualty*, and dear
Frank Williams were among them.

'OK,' announced Lin. 'Some of us will stand in a line by
the door and some of us will hide around the corner and
jump out on Chris at a given signal.'

'I don't do jumping out,' quipped the 70-year-old Frank
and we all collapsed with laughter.

We were told by Roger that Chris and Trinity had arrived
and that they were about to be brought over, still thinking
that it was a surprise party of a different kind. Chris had
been told that if he accidentally bumped into Cliff on the
way over from his room, that he could just make something
up on the spot to get him out of trouble.

Not long afterwards, I heard Chris' nervous laughter echo-
ing down the corridor. Apparently, he had indeed bumped

into Cliff in the hotel's reception area and made a dash for the nearby restaurant in the hope that he hadn't been seen. It was too late.

'Hi, Trinity, hi, Chris, what are you doing here?' we heard Cliff ask.

'Oh we're up seeing my son in Newcastle,' we heard Chris say – obviously the quickest lie he could think of.

'Well, why not join me for a drink in the next room?' said Cliff.

'We'd love to,' replied Chris, still shaken by the thought that he may have nearly given the game away.

As they came into the room with all of us standing in a line, Chris' face was a picture. He obviously thought that, by some strange chance, he was late arriving and was in danger of blowing the whole surprise. The funniest thing was when Chris attempted to get us all to sing 'Happy birthday' to Cliff and no one joined in. Poor Chris, he was totally bewildered.

Cliff then turned to Chris and said, 'Well, you think you are here because of me, but we're actually all here because of you and Christians in Entertainment.'

Chris was having none of this and could not take it in. In the end, it was Sheree who said, 'Chris, you've been gotcha-ed!'

All the other guests then appeared, including his daughter, Anna, and son, Ben, who Chris had dropped off at school that morning. His other son, Luke, was also there and, seeing them all miraculously in front of him, the realization dawned and Chris almost collapsed in a heap on to a nearby lasagne. He was totally dumbstruck.

During the party that followed, many performers, both in attendance and on a series of video snippets specially recorded by Lin throughout the year, said how helpful the work of CIE had been to them.

Chris came up to me during the evening and said, 'I saw your car in the car park.'

'Oh dear. Did it give the game away?' I asked.

'No, it was reassuring that there was going to be someone here I knew,' he said. 'Little did I think that I would actually know everyone!'

Sheree and I arrived back home very late that night, exhausted by the fun we had had, but so encouraged because so many people in the media and entertainment world had said that their Christianity is the anchor in their lives that keeps them sane and whole.

One person I had admired was dear Bryan Mosley – best known as Alf in *Coronation Street* and his role in the film *Get Carter* with Michael Caine. When the telephone rang at home, it was Sheree's mother who answered it first. She had already answered the phone to find a well-known caller a number of times before, so, in some ways, she was quite used to it. She could instantly recognize the voices of Frank Carson or Norman Collier.

'Ooooo,' she went. 'It's Alf Roberts on the phone for you, Syd!'

I'd had lots of messages via other people about Brian wanting to get in touch in the last two years or so. Brian had read my first book and then seen his own biography published and was keen to talk about our different experiences. I ended up having the most wonderful two-hour chat on the phone with him and we finished by promising each other that we would meet up. Two days later, I heard on *News at Ten* that he had died. It was terribly sad, but perhaps God had prompted him to phone me before it was too late. I shall look forward to finishing the conversation when I see him in the heaven that he so passionately believed in.

Norma, his wife, bravely did some book signings on his behalf and I met her one day when she invited me to Bryan's memorial service in Manchester. It was very strange walking in to this huge church and seeing all the characters from *Coronation Street* there. I sat down in a pew next to Bobby

Ball and immediately got a poke in the back. I turned round to see the tough guy character Jim McDonald, played by actor Charles Lawson, sitting there. He said, 'Wow! Fancy you two being sat in front of me?' He was gobsmacked to see us and we were gobsmacked to see him.

It was a lovely service, with many lovely tributes paid to Bryan, and Chris read a short extract from his biography. Afterwards I told Norma that I had to go off to Bradford to film an interview. 'I'll lead you,' she kindly offered. 'I know where the studio is.' I followed her car for several miles until she beckoned me into a side street and then waved goodbye.

As I began to look for a place to park, I heard this intense screeching sound and my heart immediately sank. 'Oh no! What's wrong with the car now?' I sighed, having just paid for it to be serviced. It sounded as if either the engine was about to explode or I had just scraped the side of the car against a wall.

When I got out of the car to investigate the noise, I suddenly realized that the sound was not coming from my car at all, but from somewhere else. I looked across the street and saw a mosque. I wasn't used to hearing the loud call to prayer that is a feature of this multicultural city and I felt utterly daft. I've laughed about my silly mistake with Norma ever since.

I've found that Christianity is not all about helping old ladies across the road and smiling all day no matter what happens, but it has made me acutely aware of other people's suffering. When a friend told me about Hannah, I knew that she could do with some extra fun and laughter in her life. She had been in Royal Liverpool Children's Hospital, Alder Hey for some time – it is a hospital that specializes in the treatment of different forms of epilepsy. I had agreed to pop along and visit her and, as I made the drive to the hospital, thoughts of my own children's suffering sprang into my mind. Then, 'How must her parents be feeling?' I pondered to myself as I walked along the hospital corridor, looking for the sign to her ward. If there was anything I could do to cheer her up, I was certainly happy to do so.

A nurse met me and told me that Hannah was quite poorly. I didn't know, she had been diagnosed with a serious viral infection that had paralyzed her from the neck down. As I walked towards the bed, I was very upset to see this 15-year-old girl lying there, attached to a strange-looking breathing machine. The nurse took it off Hannah's face so that I could talk to her and, while all this was going on, thoughts of Donna continued to come rushing back. I'm not a hospital lover at the best of times.

I needn't have worried, Hannah was lovely and she certainly didn't want anyone to feel sorry for her. She told me that she was still doing her school exams while lying there because she was keen not to allow this unexpected illness to cause her education to suffer.

As we got chatting, I looked around the walls and was struck by the number of Robbie Williams posters on the walls. When I mentioned his name, her eyes lit up and she told me that she considered herself a lifelong fan, even though she was only 15. 'Why haven't you got any pictures of Little and Large?' brought a wide grin. I sat and talked for a while longer, until I was afraid of exhausting her, then, after saying my goodbyes, left for the car park. The nurse called after me to say, 'She's a brave young girl, isn't she?'

I really felt pretty hopeless until, halfway through driving home, an idea suddenly struck me. I had met Robbie Williams' cousin, Jonathan Wilkes, during a pro-celebrity golf match earlier that year and wondered if I still had his mobile phone number in my address book at home. Jonathan, famous for being Robbie Williams' flat mate, should really be better known for all the theatre and television work that he has done in his own right – *The Rocky Horror Show* and *Godspell* to name but two very different examples.

Driving as fast as I dared, I got home and eagerly checked my records. Sure enough, I did still have Jonathan's number, but now I wondered if I had the audacity to use it and to make a very special request.

'Hiya, is that Jonathan?' I had made up my mind.

'Sure.'

'It's Syd Little here.'

'Watcha Syd! What's up?'

I explained about Hannah and asked if there was any possibility that Robbie could send a signed photo of himself to her.

'I'm sure that'll be fine,' he said. 'I'll do my best.'

A few hours later, just as I was getting ready to go out, the phone rang. I picked it up and a voice said, 'Is that Syd Little?'

I said, 'Yes', and the voice said, 'It's Robbie Williams here.'

Earlier in the day, Bobby Davro had called me and so I immediately thought it was him again, just wanting to wind me up — I simply didn't believe it was *the* Robbie Williams on the other end. Even after several minutes spent accusing him of being my mate Bobby Davro doing one of his brilliant impressions, I was still not convinced.

'No, honest, Syd. It's me, Robbie!' said the exasperated voice on the other end. Just in time, the penny dropped because Robbie mentioned that he had spoken to Jonathan and so I knew he was for real.

'No problem about sending Hannah a photo,' Robbie said. 'But I just wanted to ring you and say that you broke my dream about Little and Large.'

'Goodness me,' I said. 'Don't tell anyone otherwise your street cred will really go flying out of the window!'

After a long chat, his parting words were, 'I just wanted to say thank you for all the fun and laughter you gave me watching you on the telly while I was growing up.'

It was a very kind thing to say and I am glad to have, in

some small way, encouraged the career of someone I believe is one of the best performers of the new generation.

Later I heard about the loud whoops of delight that had been heard all over the hospital when a package of photos, CDs and books had arrived, all signed by Robbie especially for Hannah. It made my day.

12

LAUGHTER – THE BEST MEDICINE

We are a close-knit family – my in-laws live with us and we all get on very well together. 'Mum' is wonderful and 'Dad' is a very tall guy whose shoulders barely get through the doorway. When I first met him and had to ask for the hand of his daughter in marriage, he scared me to death. He is one of the most interesting people I have ever met, though. Even at nearly 80 years old, he's still building. Every time we have moved we've left a bigger house behind. In our present house, he has added a utility room, a bathroom, two bedrooms, a study with bookshelves up to the ceiling and an outside patio. You can't stop him, he's just so much happier when he's working.

The number of amazing but true stories he has told me over dinner deserve a book of their own. He was in the Royal Navy during the War and part of the Combined Operations force, a special commando service that operated well before the SAS was created. One secret mission involved a daring visit to the Greek islands of Scarpanto. The *Black Prince* was the cruiser he was aboard and from which he and his comrades were launched in flat rubber dinghies towards the shore during the cover of nightfall. Once the dinghy hit the sand, they scrambled out and hid their craft in some nearby rocks. Their mission was to discover where the Germans were positioned and morse-code this information back to the ship.

For several days their adventure caused them to hide in many different places, including a dry well where the ground shook as the German Army itself marched closely by. At one point, they were running short of food and an American pilot was used to fly over and drop them some emergency rations. As it was American, the food was less like emergency and more like luxury because they had the best rations of any army during the War. Chocolate, with sugar, cigarettes, chewing gum and soup that actually tasted of something, kept them alive while they spied on the enemy.

Once the German configurations had been sent to the captain abroad the cruiser still waiting off shore, the ship's guns started firing across to the island, right over their heads. The commandoes had to make quick their escape once they had been discovered and, at one point, were hemmed in by the Germans in a brick yard. Somehow they managed to find the dinghies and row back to the boat. It always leave me breathless when I hear Dad tell this story in full. Showbusiness has nothing on this!

Dad spent the latter years of his working life in Libya as an oilfield engineer until Colonel Gaddafi became president and ordered all the foreigners out of the country. During his time there, Dad helped build whole towns in the middle of the desert – some complete with swimming pools. He found the bones of sharks and alligators while digging in the desert, proving that it was once a sea. We still have a fossilized rose and crab from the middle of the Sahara desert sitting on our mantelpiece. We've also got a full suit of mediaeval armour standing in the hallway, but that's a different story!

I'm sometimes asked what my favourite Bible verse is. I've actually got lots of favourites because so many verses seem really apt to me. However, the one that I think would make the world a better place is from Matthew 19.19 (NRSV): '. . . "Honour your father and mother; also, you shall love your neighbour as yourself".'

'Respect' is a big word. I honestly believe that if a little more respect and love were shown by each one of us, then maybe there would be a little less hate in the world. It's also important, of course, to have respect for ourselves. Having self-respect is one way to show God that the life he has given us is something that we value. No one can be perfect of course and we all make our mistakes, but maybe we should sometimes try a little harder to get on with that person we find so difficult to cope with.

Jesus' life is full of wonderful examples of how to show respect for others. It's amazing to think that, even though he was God's son and had every right and opportunity to be proud, demanding, aggressive and controlling, he wasn't. He literally came down to our level, put himself in our shoes and showed respect for human life.

Jesus showed this respect by reminding his listeners of some of the Ten Commandments, which he quoted in the verse mentioned above. These laws were designed by God to protect people, not restrict them, as some feel today. Of course, showing respect does not mean allowing ourselves to be walked over. Jesus was able to put the pious religious leaders of his day in their proper places, but he was never aloof, he was always approachable. Jesus showed his respect for women, too, and was probably the first women's lib campaigner! Gently talking to women – who were generally seen then as much less important than men – Jesus would tell them they were important and equal in God's eyes. Jesus loved touching the ones no one else would go near and healed as many as he could physically reach. He hasn't changed today of course, but has left us the job of showing the world how much respect he has for his creation. If God respects life, so must we.

One of the greatest thrills for me in recent years is being given a lot of opportunities to share my thoughts and tell my story in so many different ways so that I can encourage others to keep going, no matter how bad things seem at the time.

It always amazes me how God has not only helped me through the ups and downs but also found a use for my experiences. One of the most memorable was when I was asked to appear for a special conference on drug abuse at a Rotary Club conference in the West Country. It was held at the huge Riviera Centre in Torquay, which was packed with people from all over the country. As I spoke about my experiences with Paul and what it was like being the parent of a drug user, I could hear a lot of gasps going on in the audience. When I stepped down from the stage and away from the glare of the lights, I could see a lot of other people could relate to my story. I'm glad it touched them and I hope it brought them some encouragement, too.

I know that the gospel shows, videos, articles and tapes that I have done have also provided some extra hope for others who may be going through tough times. After my first autobiography (HarperCollins, 1999, *Little Goes a Long Way*), I was pleased to be able to offer an introduction for Chris' *Long Hot Soak* series, which is full of stories of hope and triumph over adversity. When it was suggested that I co-compile a book containing my favourite church-based jokes, I jumped at the chance. After all, I've based my whole career on making people laugh. Out of the many funny stories in *The Little Book of Heavenly Humour* (Canterbury Press, 2002) I have two favourites:

> One small child knelt by the side of his bed and prayed, 'Dear God, you know that the Bible says that you come from dust and go to dust? Well, come and have a look under my bed, because someone's either coming or going! Amen.'

> Little Tim was in the garden filling in a hole when his neighbour peered over the fence.

Interested in what the cheeky-faced youngster was up to, he politely asked, 'What are you up to there, Tim?'

'My goldfish died,' replied Tim tearfully, without looking up, 'and I've just had a funeral service before burying him.'

The neighbour was concerned. 'That's an awfully big hole for a goldfish, isn't it?'

Tim patted down the last heap of earth then replied, 'That's because he's inside your stupid cat.'

I do love making people laugh and, in these worrying days, it seems to be more important than ever because I think that laughter goes much deeper than we think. I believe that what I said in the Introduction to my book *The Little Book of Heavenly Humour*, is so important that I make no apology for re-emphasizing it here because, having a good laugh each day could actually increase your life expectancy. Music can sweep through the spirit and bring tranquillity to the soul, while drama sharpens the emotions and challenges the brain. Laughter, on the other hand, is God's perfect medicine.

Why do I think laughter is so important? Well, here follow 11 good reasons of my own.

For a start, laughter is God's special provision for us. We are the only being he created that has the ability to laugh. Tigers, elephants, ants, gnus and even laughing hyenas can't actually titter, gurgle and hoot like we can. This must mean that it's a special gift from God and if we just leave it unopened in its box, we are doing ourselves and him a disservice. We're also missing out on something that makes us feel good.

Then I believe that laughter is certainly God's medicine, put on this Earth to help ease the pain of everyday life. Standing on stage hearing all the laughter is the most wonderful feeling. On days when I have been unwell, yet abided by the old adage 'the show must go on', the laughter coming from the audience has made me feel a whole lot better. As we give out the laughter medicine to the audience, they give it back with their response. I can even get a little high on the laughter.

Laughter can turn tears of sadness into cries of joy, heaviness of heart into happiness of spirit and, in the middle of our difficulties, remind us that life really does go on. Even the top medical scientists now claim that a good chortle has an enormous effect on the way we live our lives. There is medical and scientific evidence to prove that laughter is good for us. Apparently, it increases the amount of oxygen in the blood, which helps the body to heal itself and resist further infection. It also lowers the heart rate, stimulates the appetite and burns up calories. A good laugh will also stimulate the body's natural pain-killing tranquillizers, beta-endorphins, leading some experts to suggest that laughing can prevent ulcers and digestive disorders.

A leading French neurologist has studied laughter and concluded that one minute of laughter provides up to 45 minutes of subsequent relaxation. Another medical scientist recently reported that, 'People who regularly exercise their face muscles can expect to delay middle-aged sagging for at least ten years.'

It's also good exercise because your whole body has to join in. If you see anyone trying to laugh with just their lips, it looks like they've swallowed a bumble bee. Dr William Fry, a professor at Stanford Medical School, says, '100 laughs a day gives you as much beneficial exercise as 10 minutes of rowing'.

Laughter also breaks down all the barriers of race, age, gender and creed. It's designed for everybody to enjoy!

It's also made for sharing. A laugh with a friend can be a very bonding experience and, if you accidentally giggle in the middle of an argument, it has the effect of stopping the quarrel instantaneously. All the animosity can disappear in one moment. Have you ever been in a theatre where someone is laughing louder than everyone else? I love it when I'm doing a show and someone has a loud and perhaps raucous laugh, because very soon everyone is laughing at the one who is laughing loudest! Laughter is contagious.

I remember Fiona Castle saying, 'The encouraging times were when my husband Roy was ill but was able to laugh at his illness rather than let it overcome him. So it is in life, it's often the difficult things that we laugh at later. If life really goes smoothly, you've actually got nothing to look back on and laugh at.'

I agree with Fiona and remember that when we were filming some sketches for our *The Little & Large Show* for the BBC, it was always the unintentional events that caused the film crew to crack up the most.

In a world of great pressure and uncertainty, laughter provides a unique way of switch off from life's everyday burdens. So, it's a natural stress reliever. It's not a way of running away from problems as most jokes are focused on the nature of humanity itself. The slip on the banana skin, the mistake that someone made and the silly situations we find ourselves in become the focus of our amusement. Humour can help us face our fears and see things as they really are, providing us with an uncharacteristic armour of confidence.

No wonder we all have comedy heroes because comedians down the ages have devoted their lives to making people laugh and have known the secret of laughter for years. From the clown in the circus to the comedy scriptwriter, from the mediaeval jester hired for the king to famous comics such as Tommy Cooper and Les Dawson, Ken Dodd and Morecambe and Wise – all have shown us that a good giggle is an essential element in our daily lives.

I wonder who your comedy hero is? What is it that makes you laugh out loud? Whatever it is, try to get as much of it as you can because it will do you good. Harry Secombe said, 'I think you can laugh at almost anything, so long as it doesn't hurt anybody.' So there must be a lot of laughter material to choose from and if there isn't a shortage let's take God's special gift seriously.

If you were offered a pill in Boots that took away stress, brought you closer to others, stopped painful arguments, healed you, killed pain, helped you relax, boosted your immune system, helped prevent stomach disorders, exercised you, helped prevent worry and stopped your skin from sagging, I have no doubt that you would take it at least three times a day!

When I am invited to talk about my own personal struggles and how my faith helped me through, I ensure that laughter always has a central role in the evening. Those mirthmakers whose job it is to create amusement have been entrusted with a seriously important task. My good friends Cannon and Ball, Jimmy Cricket and Don Maclean recently joined me in making a video called *The Laughter Makers*. In it they talked about how seriously they take the job and privilege of making people laugh. As Thomas Merton put it, 'Clowns and comedians are likely to have a high place in heaven as they must be near the heart of God.'

When I appeared as a special guest with Cannon and Ball on their 'Rock Around the Church' tour in October 2003, I thought it would be just a one-off event. However, the show has proved time and again that laughter and faith go so well together and are needed in many of our churches across the UK that we are now planning a third tour and it looks set to run for some time to come. I really can't wait for my next chance to get up there and hear an audience laughing wherever it is. I've been doing it for so long, how can I stop now?

Does God laugh? The Bible says, Being cheerful keeps you healthy. It is slow death to be gloomy all the time. We are also told that God laughs, particularly at the wicked and their feeble plans. In Ecclesiastes we read that there is a time to weep and a time to laugh. Even dear, suffering Job longs for the day when God will fill his mouth with laughter once more.

I'm sure that for Jesus to hold an audience of over 5000 men, women and children all day, he must have used humour as a vehicle to get his point across at least some of the time. We remember what we laugh at, too, because a joke demands a response. Jesus was an expert at driving home his points with terrifically funny jokes of the day. I wonder if the disciples were the original Crazy Gang or Riding Lights Theatre Company? Did they engender hoots of mirth as they enacted the story of the man trying to get a speck of dust out of his brother's eye while being unable to see the log sticking out of his own?

The Bible says that we should have the attitude of little children in order to enter heaven. Whenever I am with children, they seem to spend most of their time laughing and giggling. Research shows that they spend more time laughing than the average adult, so perhaps we should take a leaf out of their book.

We're pretty adept at judging each other in church, so maybe we could practise changing our negativity for humour a little more often. I heard a story about a couple who were on the way home from church, standing at the bus stop waiting in the torrential rain for over half an hour. Finally, they decided to pray for help. It was good to put into practice what the sermon had been about that morning, they decided. Bowing their heads and closing their eyes, they began to focus their thoughts directly heavenward. As they prayed with outright fervour and confidence, they didn't hear or see the bus arrive, stop and then promptly leave without them. Opening their eyes just in time to see it pull away round the corner, they elbowed each other back into consciousness as they suddenly remembered the dual command from Jesus in Mark 13 – he said '*watch* and pray'!

Of course, there are different kinds of laughter. The laugh bellowed in scorn does not have the same birthplace as a laugh of fun and jollity. Like everything in God's perfect creation, laughter can be twisted and used to bring harm rather than healing. God used his words to create the world in Genesis, so let's use our words to build up rather than tear down. Perhaps the main issue is to laugh with someone rather than at them. Laughter has been given to us as a tool of communication, not as a way to hurt someone.

Similarly, we should not find ourselves laughing at God, but recognize that he laughs at our crazy attempts to subdue life, while still loving us deeply. Ultimately, God's desire is for our laughter to be the outward expression of the deep love and security we can experience from him. While we should not expect to be bubbling with superficial laughter all the time, every true Christian can be full of deep joy.

Laughter can be a reminder to take our faith seriously, but not ourselves. Being a serious bunch, we could do with reminding ourselves that it's important to see the funny side of our faith and our problems from time to time. Let's not make fun of each other, but instead encourage one another to giggle and see God chuckle with us.

I would urge you to make sure that you take your dose of laughter medicine every day. I hope that this book has made you laugh, too, and see that there is more to life than what you see in front of your nose.

You will have noticed that this book has the title *Little by Little*. Apart from the play on my name, I have found that this is the best way to deal with life – the good and the bad. There are lots of sayings such as 'Don't bite off more than you can chew' or 'Too much of anything is bad for you' that just help to underline my point that we should just take things as they come. When the Bible says, Don't worry about tomorrow because today has enough worries of its own, I couldn't agree more.

Another reason for this title is that God has been extremely patient with me and let me come back to him little by little. In turn, instead of waving some huge celestial magic wand and turning me into a perfect Christian, if there is such a thing, he has slowly shown me how my life can be different. Little by little I have come through all the ups and downs of my professional and personal life and these experiences have made me a richer and deeper man.

I'm glad that, within all the madness of showbiz, I have managed to keep my feet on the ground and do the decorating and pull my family around me. I've always been me. I've enjoyed every moment as special. I have never regretted anything I have done in my life. Now I realize that I am being guided and, whatever happens, this will see me through.

What will my epitaph be? Perhaps, 'He never got to sing a song on his own'. I would have to reply from my grave, 'Oh yes he did!' This is because, as I explained earlier, one of the songs I use to finish my gospel gigs is the one made famous by Daniel O'Donnell. It's based on the famous 'Footprints' poem, about someone questioning God about the fact that there are two sets of footprints in the sand apart from the really bad times when there is just one set.

'Why did you leave me when I needed you most?' the person asks.

God explains that when the person needed him most, God carried them – the single set of footprints in the sand are God's. This is why I sing this song to finish, because it sums up my spiritual life and experience so well.

> Footsteps walking with me
> Footsteps I cannot see
> But every move I make
> And every step I take
> I know they're there with me
> They walk with me all the way

Beside me day by day
Through good and bad
Through happy and sad
Those footsteps won't go away.

I'll never walk in life alone
There'll always be someone there
I know he won't let me down
He's with me everywhere
The special things in life I've done
Have been through him and his love
I've been blessed in so many ways
Thanks to the Lord above.

Footsteps walking with me
Footsteps I cannot see
But every move I make
And every step I take
I know they're there with me
They walk with me all the way
Beside me day by day
Through good and bad
Through happy and sad
Those footsteps won't go away.

I think that my life's been planned
By the one who's guiding me
When I'm led by the hand
Of someone I can't see
I'm not always sure where to go
That's when I follow his lead
I know that the pathway that he shows
Will help me to succeed.

Footsteps walking with me
Footsteps I cannot see
But every move I make
And every step I take
I know they're there with me
They walk with me all the way
Beside me day by day
Through good and bad
Through happy and sad
By my side they will stay.

Well, I always think that there are three ways in which an autobiographist (that's a big word isn't it? In fact I just made it up, but it sounds OK!) can finish a book. There are those who tell their whole life in ten chapters and then spend the next three padding things out with a collection of completely unconnected, haphazard stories. Then there are those who bring everything absolutely bang up to date, almost as if to suggest that their life ends there and that nothing else is likely to happen. The ones I favour, though, are those who almost seem to end in mid sentence. The river is still flowing and there's plenty more to come. That's me. I feel I've only just started my new career and I can't wait to see what's around the corn . . .

Keep laughing!

FUNNY 'LITTLE' QUOTES TO MAKE YOU THINK

Over the years, I have collected many quotes that include my surname, as playing on the word 'little' holds some intrigue for me. Here are just a few examples.

If you add a little to a little, and then do it again, soon that little shall be much.

Hesiod, c. eighth century B C, Greek didactic

They shifted a little, but not to return my stare.

Elizabeth Bishop (1911–79), poet

He knows little, who will tell his wife all he knows.

Thomas Fuller (1608–61), British cleric

He who sees little always sees a little less; he who hears badly always hears a little more.

Friedrich Nietzsche (1844–1900)

Thank heaven for little girls! For little girls get bigger every day.

Alan Jay Lerner (1918–86)

Have yourself a merry little Christmas, make the Yuletide gay.

Ralph Blane (b. 1914)

Time for a little something.

A. A. Milne (1882–1956), author of Winnie-the-Pooh

There is nothing, sir, too little for so little a creature as man. It is by studying little things that we attain the great art of having as little misery and as much happiness as possible.

Samuel Johnson (1709–84), author

From you, Ianthe, little troubles pass like little ripples down a sunny river.

Walter Savage Landor (1775–1864), poet

At 60, I know little more about wisdom than I did at 30, but I know a great deal more about folly.

Mason Cooley (b. 1927)

How far that little candle throws his beams! So shines a good deed in a naughty world.

William Shakespeare (1564–1616), playwright

There is very little difference between men and women in space.

Helen Sharman (b. 1963), astronaut

There are no little events in life, those we think of no consequence may be full of fate, and it is at our own risk if we neglect the acquaintances and opportunities that seem to be casually offered, and of small importance.

Amelia E. Barr (1831–1919), author

To touch God a little with our mind is a great blessing, to grasp him is impossible.

St Augustine (354–430)

The taking of a little prize, do not a single heart despise.

Aurelian Townshend (c. 1583–c. 1651), poet

Forgive, O Lord, my little jokes on thee, and I'll forgive thy great big one on me.

Robert Frost (1874–1963), poet

What we call little things are merely the causes of great things; they are the beginning, the embryo, and it is the point of departure which, generally speaking, decides the whole future of an existence. One single black speck may be the beginning of gangrene, of a storm, of a revolution.

Henri-Frédéric Amiel (1821–81), Swiss philosopher

Those who know much talk little; those who know little talk much.

Chinese proverb

O little town of Bethlehem,
How still we see thee lie!
Above they deep and dreamless sleep
The silent stars go by;

Yet in thy dark streets shineth
The everlasting Light;
The hopes and fears of all the years
Are met in thee tonight.

Phillips Brooks (1835–93), clergyman

Whoever is faithful in a very little is faithful also in much; and whoever is dishonest in a very little is dishonest also in much.

Matthew 25.21

Mary had a little lamb, its fleece was white as snow, and everywhere that Mary went the lamb was sure to go.

Sarah Josepha Buell Hale (1788–1879), author

Society needs to condemn a little more and understand a little less.

John Major (b. 1943), former British Prime Minister

Those who have seen little wonder a lot.

Chinese proverb

We say little, when vanity does not make us speak.

Attributed to François, Duc De La Rochefoucauld (1613–80), writer

Wine is a little like love; when the right one comes along, you know it.

Bolla Wines

Little Boy kneels at the foot of the bed
Droops on the little hands, little gold head;
Hush! Hush! Whisper who dares!
Christopher Robin is saying his prayers.

A. A. Milne (1882–1956), author of Winnie-the-Pooh

Do you know that a little yeast leavens the whole batch of dough?

1 Corinthians 5.6

Man was kreated a little lower than the angels and has bin gittin a little lower ever sinse.

Josh Billings [Henry Wheeler Shaw] (1818–85), humorist

Grown-up people do very little and say a great deal. Toddlers say very little and do a great deal.

Penelope Leach, child development specialist

There was a little man, and he had a little soul; And he said, Little Soul, let us try, try, try!

Thomas Moore (1779–1852), musician and songwriter

If I only had a little humility, I'd be perfect.

Ted Turner

I am a little pencil in the hand of a writing God who is sending a love letter to the world.

Mother Teresa

Drink no longer water, but use a little wine for thy stomach's sake.

1 Timothy 5.23

They came, they saw, they did a little shopping.

Graffiti on the Berlin Wall

To remain mysterious, say little and do nothing.

Mason Cooley (b. 1927), aphorist

Little drops of water, little grains of sand, make the mighty ocean and the beauteous land.

Julia A. Fletcher Carney (1824–1908)

I know what it is to have little, and I know what it is to have plenty. In any and all circumstances I have learned the secret of being well-fed and of going hungry, of having plenty and of being in need. I can do all things through him who strengthens me.

Philippians 4.13

Wealth hastily gotten will dwindle, but whose who gather little by little will increase it.

Proverbs 13.11

Our knowledge is a little island in a great ocean of non-knowledge.

Isaac Bashevis, singer

When I grow up I want to be a little boy.

Joseph Heller (1923–), novelist

Little deeds of kindness, little words of love, help to make Earth happy like the heaven above.

Julia A. Fletcher Carney (1824–1908)

Away in a manger, no crib for a bed,
The little Lord Jesus laid down his sweet head.
The stars in the bright sky looked down where he lay –
The little Lord Jesus asleep in the hay.

Martin Luther (1483–1546), religious leader

'Well, I should like to be a little larger, sir, if you wouldn't mind,' said Alice: 'three inches is such a wretched height to be.'

Lewis Carroll (1832–98), author

Among most Christians the Old Testament is little read in comparison to the New Testament.

Erich Fromm (1900–80), psychologist

It is explained that all relationships require a little give and take. This is untrue. Any partnership demands that we give and give and give . . .

Quentin Crisp (b. 1908), author

It is normal to give away a little of one's life in order not to lose it all.

Albert Camus (1913–60), philosopher and author

I'll tell you one thing. If a little green man pops out at me I'm shooting first and asking questions later.

Edward D. Wood, Jr (1922–78), director, screenwriter

A little group of wise hearts is better than a wilderness of fools.

John Ruskin (1819–1900), art and social critic

A little learning is a dangerous thing.

Alexander Pope (1688–1744), poet

What could be wanting . . . but to have wrote a book. Little boots it to the subtle speculatist to stand single in his opinions – unless he gives them proper vent.

Laurence Sterne (1713–68), author and clergyman

Love me little, love me long.

Christopher Marlowe (1564–93), playwright and poet

Never in the history of fashion has so little material been raised so high to reveal so much that needs to be covered.

Cecil Beaton (1904–80), photographer and designer

Truly I tell you, whoever does not receive the kingdom of God as a little child will never enter it.

Mark 10.15

It has long been an axiom of mine that the little things are infinitely the most important.

Sir Arthur Conan Doyle (1859–1930), author

He that considers how little he dwells upon the condition of others, will learn how little the attention of others is attracted by himself.

Samuel Johnson (1709–84), author

'Why are you afraid, you of little faith?' Then he got up and rebuked the winds and the sea; and there was a dead calm.

Matthew 14.31

A little meat best fits a little belly,
As sweetly Lady, give me leave to tell ye,
This little Pipkin fits this little Jelly

Robert Herrick (1591–1674), poet

A little grit in the eye destroyeth the sight of the very heavens, and a little malice or envy a world of joys.

Thomas Traherne (1636–74), clergyman

Little Boy Blue, Come blow your horn.

Traditional Nursery rhyme

This little world, this little state, this little commonwealth of our own.

Woodrow Wilson (1856–1924), American president

A little knowledge that acts is worth infinitely more than much knowledge that is idle.

Kahlil Gibran (1883–1931), poet

That little kiss you stole held all my heart and soul.

Frank Loesser (1910–69), songwriter

The great rule: if the little bit you have is nothing special in itself, at least find a way of saying it that is a little bit special.

G. C. Lichtenberg (1724–99), physicist

Little by little the pieces and squares began to come to life.

Vladimir Nabokov (1899–1977), novelist

So, it all just goes to show that life should not be rushed. It's best just taken a day at a time, little by little!